Stopmotion Explosion

Stopmotion Explosion

Animate ANYTHING and Make MOVIES

Epic films for $20 or less
This book will show you how

Check out our free downloads and
additional resources online!
www.stopmotionexplosion.com

Nate Eckerson
PO Box 967, North Dighton, MA 02764

First Edition: March 2011

ISBN 978-0-9833311-0-0

Computers : Digital Media - Video & Animation
Performing Arts : Animation
Performing Arts : Film & Video - Amateur Production

Book & cover design by Nate Eckerson
Storyboard (pg. 58) & Fight Arc (pg. 154) illustrations by Mark Eckerson

*To my parents and siblings for their never-ending support
and my filmmaking mentors*

Contents

Chapter 1

Horse Hooves, Paintings and How Movies Work

Anyone can get their hands on a camcorder. They're simple to use. Hit the red button, record some footage, download the video, click play, and there's Uncle Bob singing karaoke at Aunt Clarissa's 50th birthday party.

Later, you join a video chat with the family in Indiana and send them the video, so they can laugh too.

We're surrounded by movies. Internet video, TV programs, Dvds, video games, even roadside billboards grab drivers with moving images. We're so accustomed to watching life on screens that the weirdness has been lost.

The biggest obstacle to understanding stopmotion is found in our preconceived notions about movies. People find stopmotion difficult to grasp because they think they understand how movies work.

"Movies show moving things moving."

Is this true? Sometimes.

Wires? Greenscreen? CGI?

When people see toys, models, and impossible things come to life, movies become weird again. The audience thinks the creators used special effects, invisible wires, computerized 3D models, or maybe they erased their fingers out of the video using that greenscreen stuff. *Amazing what you can do with computers these days, buddy.* This might be your perception too.

The Epsom Derby, (1821)

As you'll discover in this book, stopmotion is much simpler, and uses none of the techniques above. In fact, stopmotion has been in existence almost as long as movies themselves.

The key to understanding stopmotion is understanding what movies really are, and how they trick our eyes into seeing motion. To help you understand how this is possible, we'll take a little trip through movie history.

A Short History of Film

Before the photograph was invented, artists captured the world around them in sketches, pastels, oils, and other mediums. Horses were strong, beautiful subjects, requiring a bold hand, but artists could never agree about one thing. Did all four of a horse's hooves leave the ground during a gallop? Jean Louis Théodore Géricault thought they did, and he painted *The Epsom Derby* this way in 1821.

Photography was invented in the early 1800s. The process used a flat surface covered with chemicals that changed colors when exposed to light. One of the earliest photographs surviving to the present was taken by artist Joseph Nicéphore Niépce in 1827. It's a picturesque image of a barn roof and some walls, the view from his window. The camera had to sit in the window for eight hours before an image was traced in the photographic chemicals by the sun. It was some time before the chemical formulas improved, and photos could capture a moving object without the image blurring into mush.

Meanwhile, horse-racing aristocrats were galloping about England, commissioning artists to paint their favorite mounts. John Frederick Herring thought all four hooves of the Newmarket steeds left the ground too. He painted the winning gallop of the steed Priam like this:

'Priam' beating Lord Exeter's 'Augustus' at Newmarket, (1831)

Inventors were making progress in other fields. In London during the 1820s, it was discovered that painting images, one on each side of a card, suspending the card between two strings and spinning the card rapidly would combine the two images. The toy was named Thaumatrope, from the Greek for "wonder turner." It's very easy to make a Thaumatrope. Can you invent a design of your own?

Roughly ten years later, the Zoetrope was invented. Several pictures of an object in motion were printed on a strip of paper and placed inside a circular drum with slits cut in the sides. By spinning the drum and looking through the slits, the viewer saw a flickering, looping image that appeared to move. The name "Zoetrope" is derived from the Greek for "wheel of life." Today, we call this illusion of movement "Persistence of Vision."

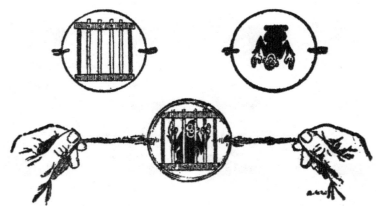

Artists were still debating horses. In 1872, Leland Stanford, former governor of California, horse racing man and railroad tycoon made a bet with photographer Eadweard Muybridge intending to answer the question forever. Do all four hooves of a galloping horse leave the ground at once?

Muybridge placed several cameras around a racetrack, stretching wires attached to the cameras' shutters across the horse's path. As the horse galloped past, the wires broke, triggering each camera in succession.

The Zoetrope

The series of pictures proved that all four hooves do leave the ground. History was made, Muybridge won the bet, and artists, including Edgar Degas studied the images closely, using them to improve their paintings and sculptures.

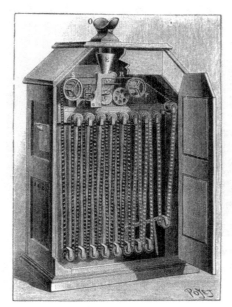

In 1889, Thomas Edison, was given a roll of George Eastman's newly invented flexible photographic film. Edison had seen Muybridge's work, and was developing a moving picture device in collaboration with Edison Labs photographer William Dickson. Edison saw how a long row of pictures printed on the new film could be shown to a viewer, one picture at a time,

The Kinetoscope

Le cinématographe Lumière: projection.

The Cinématographe in projector mode. Note the hand-turned crank feeding a spool of film in front of the light. The light source, a bright arc lamp, is focused on the film with a series of lenses. The light passes through the transparent film, projecting the image onto a screen. (Mustache optional).

using a system of rollers, a crank, and a peephole in the top of a box. As the viewer turned the crank and looked into the box, the pictures flashing past appeared to move, thanks to the persistence of vision effect discovered by inventors of the Thaumatrope and Zoetrope.

This device, which Edison named the Kinetoscope, became very popular. Audiences lined up outside Kinetoscope parlors, and George Eastman's Kodak film became the basis of a whole new moving picture industry.

In 1895 the Lumière Brothers, Aguste and Louis revealed their Cinématographe, a device that captured a series of images on a strip of film, developed the film, then projected the image on a screen by shining a bright light through the clear film. This was the first modern film projector.

Edison followed this invention with the Vitascope, the first commercially successful projector in the United States. This was the beginning of the movie theater industry as we know it today.

A strip of film. Each picture is one "frame."

Stopmotion

In 1896, James Stuart Blackton was experimenting with the stop-action movie technique. It was a simple way to create basic special effects. The camera would record a portion of film, then stop. Everyone froze in place while an actor ran off screen. After the actor disappeared, the camera restarted and the remaining actors pretended to be amazed. To the audience sitting in the theater, it looked like the actor had suddenly vanished.

After starting and stopping the camera several times, Blackton noticed clouds drifting across the background of the scene looked funny. He decided to replicate the comic effect in new films. Eventually, he discovered that starting and stopping the camera in tiny increments, one picture, or "frame" at a time and moving an object between frames created the illusion of motion.

One of Blackton's first films created with this technique, *Humorous Phases of Funny Faces* (1906), was a series of chalk drawings on a blackboard. Between frames, Blackton erased, or added a new lines

Humorous Phases of Funny Faces, (1906)

to the drawings, creating characters that smiled, blinked, and smoked cigars.

Puppet Animation

Blackton progressed to creating short films with small puppets. The puppet was moved in little increments. Each time the puppet moved, a picture was taken of its new position.

Stopmotion puppets can be very complex. Skeletons, called armatures, are made out of thin, flexible materials. Wire, or rods of metal ending in ball joints and special connectors are used. Clay, foam, rubber, fabric, and other materials are wrapped around this skeleton, until it looks like a character.

King Kong, (1931). He's a lot tamer when you realize all that gorilla muscle is a bunch of rubber and rabbit fur, about 18 inches high. This said, Kong is more than a match for a rubber pterodactyl.

In the US, movies with hand-drawn animation (like Blackton's *Humorous Phases*) became more popular than stopmotion using puppets. Stopmotion became a technique used mainly to create special effects in live-action films. The work of Willis O'Brien, an early effects animator can be seen in movies like *King Kong* (1933). The rise of stopmotion's popularity can been seen in early TV shows for kids. *Gumby* (1953) and *Davey and Goliath* (1960) are two well-known examples.

Stopmotion films remain popular today. Movies like *Wallace and Gromit: The Curse of the Were Rabbit* (2005), *Chicken Run* (2000), *Fantastic Mr. Fox* (2009), and others have proved audiences' taste for the unique look and storytelling opportunities that stopmotion offers. Additionally, hundreds of people are discovering the simplicity and flexibility of stopmotion while creating movies with their own computers and cameras. That's what this book is about!

The Skinny on Armatures

Figures constructed around armatures have a long, proud history in the stopmotion world. Armatures used in feature films and TV series are constructed solidly. Built with machined metal ball-and-socket joints, a large, custom-made armature can cost upwards of four figures. Kit-made armatures cost less, but are still expensive, running around $150 to $300 each.

If you'd like to build your own armature, it would be best to start with a wire and Epoxy-putty model, as pictured here. These are simple and cheap to make.

The wire used in this armature is heavy gauge aluminum wire. It's flexible, light, and quite strong, but has a tendency to break if nicked, so be careful while forming your figure.

The "bones" of the armature are made of Epoxy putty, a strong, self-hardening material that can be purchased at most hardware stores. The putty prevents the wire from becoming unwound, and gives the figure joints, allowing repeatable movements.

The feet are made from small pieces of plywood with two holes drilled in each piece. The armature's leg-wires are inserted into the first hole in the foot and epoxied into place. The second hole, which goes all the way through the foot, is used to anchor the armature in place while animating. Finally, the body of the figure, made from clay, foam, cotton, or latex is modeled around the armature.

Project: Building an Armature

Want to start animating with an armature? Follow these step-by-step instructions and roll your own.

Materials

- 16-18 gage aluminum wire
- Epoxy putty
- Epoxy glue
- Small piece of 3/4" plywood

Tools

- Handheld electric drill
- Vise (or pliers, and someone to hold them)
- Wire cutters

Aluminum wire can be inexpensively purchased online. If you're a scavenger type, aluminum wire can be found inside heavy-duty electrical wiring. We recommend 16-18 gage wire. Use thinner wire for smaller armatures.

Cut off a four foot section of wire. Bend the wire in the middle, so the two ends meet. Stick the bent end into the bit holder of an electric drill.

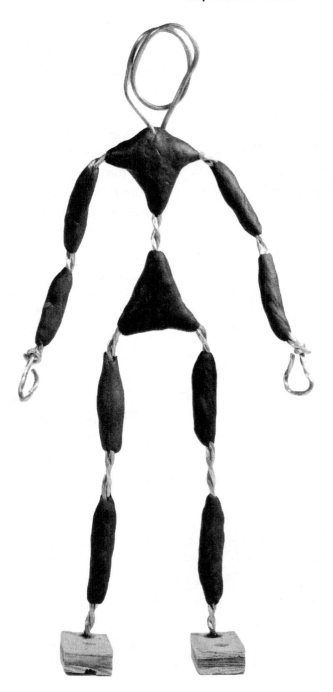

Tighten the bit holder until the wire is held fast. Clamp the two loose wire ends in a vise. Pull the wire straight, and run the drill slowly. The two strands of wire should twist together.

Using wire cutters and pliers, form the wire into the shapes pictured here. Wrap the wires together, into the shape of your figure.

Cut two 3/4" x 1-1/2" pieces of plywood. Drill a hole halfway through one end of the first piece of wood. The size of your drill bit should be

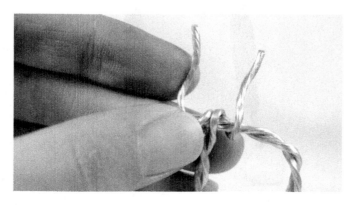

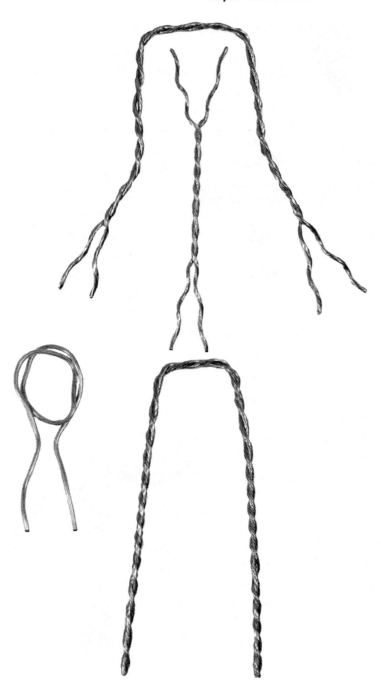

large enough so that your twisted wire fits snugly inside the hole, in this example we used a 5/32" bit. (All measurements can be fudged as needed for your project!)

Drill a second, 1/4" hole completely through the other end of the wood. This hole will be used to fasten the armature to the animating surface. (Use the picture of the armature foot as a reference while drilling your holes). Repeat, drilling two holes in the second piece of wood.

Dip the two wire "legs" of the armature into epoxy glue, and insert into the two half-drilled holes. Apply more glue as needed. Allow the glue to dry.

Mix your epoxy putty, following the instructions on the container. Use the putty to form the armature's "bones." Allow the putty to harden.

Finish the armature by bending the ends of the "arm" wires into small loops, as pictured.

Using a bolt and nut, the armature can be fastened to any surface with holes in it (for example, a piece of pegboard used for hanging tools)

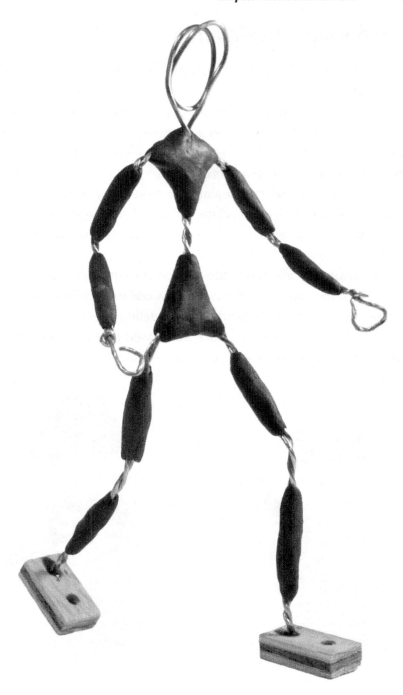

Introducing... The Minifig!

We have a special affinity for films made with toys, particularly LEGO® bricks and minifigs.

Minifigs have 7 movable joints, a nice middle ground between complex, many-jointed armatures (King Kong) and jointless toys (green army men). Minifigs also come with a wide range of facial expressions, a great way to give your characters emotion.

The studs on a LEGO® baseplate are a great way to measure your minifig movements. The baseplate will also hold the minifig in place while you animate. Balance is one of the more challenging aspects of stopmotion.

A professional, all-metal stop-motion armature can cost around $300 dollars. You can buy minifigs for a few dollars each, and they come with plenty of detailed accessories. No modeling experience required!

You can buy minifigs and LEGO® sets based on TV and movies, like Indiana Jones and Star Wars™ and SpongeBob Squarepants™ *(yeah, whatever)*.

Introducing... The Stikfa!

Stikfas are another small, inexpensive, super-poseable figure with interchangeable parts and plenty of accessories. Stikfas have been designed in a way that makes them perfect for animating.

Depending on the model, a basic Stikfa figure has three or four arm and leg joints, a waist joint, and neck joint, for a total of 14-18 movable joints. Compare this to the seven joints LEGO® minifigs have. Stikfas are a great way to increase the complexity and realism of your animations.

Stikfas can be balanced in all kinds of crazy positions, as pictured here. (Sticking a little piece of double-sided tape on the bottom of a Stikfa's foot is an easy, invisible way to give the figure more grip).

Themed Stikfa sets come with characters from history, careers, sports, military, and science fiction.

Stikfas come with a page of "stikers" that can be applied to the figure, like military belts, or a set of ninja eyes. Stikfas can be painted, sanded, drilled, and combined with other Stikfa sets, allowing the creation of truly unique characters.

Stikfas and LEGO® minifigs are just two of many toys, models and figures that can star in an animated film. Look for jointed figures that hold a pose, are easy to balance and adjust, and come with accessories that can be used as props.

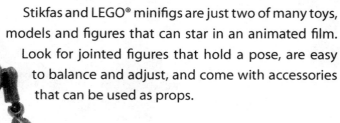

Other Methods

Most of the animating techniques we cover in this book apply to puppet and object animation. Other forms of stopmotion exist. We encourage you to investigate them. All of these methods can be combined in weird, wonderful ways.

Papermation

Sometimes called "cutout animation" papermation is made with flat materials. The camera is suspended directly above a table, pointing downward. Photos, newspaper and magazine cutouts, characters made from cardstock, construction paper and such are placed on the table and animated.

A cutout animation can be enhanced by drawing on the table surface around the cutouts, similar to the method James Blackton used to animate *Humorous Phases of Funny Faces*. To give a very simple example, if you animated a car pulling away from a stop sign, you could draw some skid marks behind it.

For Example...

This cutout rocket, made with sissors, construction paper, gluesticks, and markers has three stages of construction-paper rocket-engine power!

- When the rocket is going fast, the largest stage is placed on the end. When the rocket is decending slowly into a lunar crater, the smallest stage is used.

With a little cotton wool spread beneath the rocket, "smoke" caused by the rocket exhaust can be animated. Liftoff!

Feel free to trace and copy the rocket for use in your own projects. Or create a design of your own!

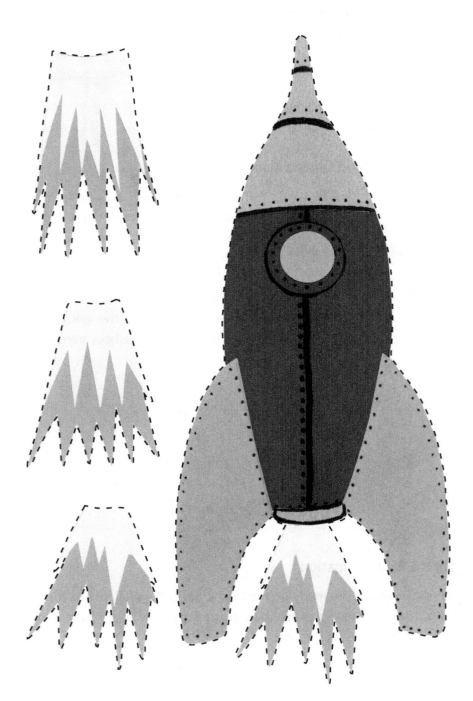

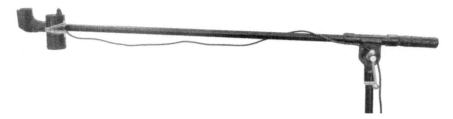

Project: Overhead Camera Mount

You can pick up an inexpensive microphone stand for around $20-40 dollars. These make great, flexible small-camera mounts when working with cutouts, or a lightbox.

In this example, a small webcamera has been attached to the end of the stand with a bunch of rubber bands.

Sand & Paint Animation

Sand animations are made on top of a "lightbox", a shallow box topped with a semi-opaque material, like frosted glass or paper, that allows diffused light to pass through.

This lightbox was built with four pieces of scrap plywood and a couple of sheets of waxed paper stretched tightly across the top. Paper is cheap, but if you're doing a lot of animation, purchase a square piece of white Plexiglas and place it over the box. Plexiglas is durable, easy to work on, and since the white Plexiglas diffuses, or "spreads out" the light, the paper isn't needed.

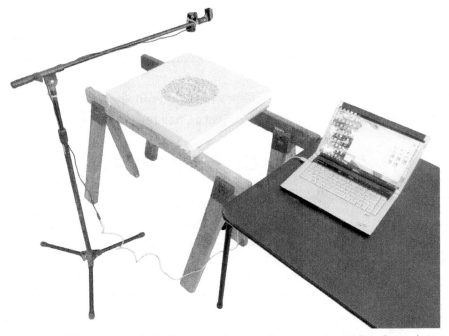

Simple lightbox setup. The light source (a scoop lamp, as pictured in the Lighting chapter) is placed on the floor, under the lightbox. The lightbox is resting on a couple of sawhorses.

As with paper animation, a camera is positioned over the box pointing downwards. Sand is visible as a black shadow on top of the lightbox. The sand is animated by pushing it into new shapes. Any fine-grained material can be used in place of sand. Try kitty litter, bird seed, or fine-grained pasta. A paintbrush is handy for brushing the sand across the top of the box.

Paint animation is very similar. Slow-drying oil paint is spread and animated on a glass surface. A lightbox with a glass top can be used for paint animation.

People Animation

People act like living armatures, moving one frame at a time in sync with the camera. Interacting with your animated characters is a basic application of this technique. Animate a giant hand reaching into a scene and grabbing something, or being attacked by a mob of plastic green army men.

As mentioned in the example box here, you can animate entire films by poising people and immobile objects. Chair races anyone?

For Example...

If you have a digital camera, check to see if it has a "sports" setting, used to photograph action without the picture blurring.

Photograph someone jumping into the air repeatedly. Take pictures when the person is at the top of their jump, knees tucked under them. After jumping, the subject should walk forward one step and jump again.

String the photos together (either flip through the pictures using the camera's image preview, or use a program like VirtualDub).

If done correctly, it will look like the person is hovering around the yard, knees under them.

A Word about Computers

You'll be running video and image editing programs. These require more memory and resources than a text editor, but your system does not need to be a supercomputer. Here are our recommended computer specs.

Windows Minimum Requirements

- **Operating System**: Windows XP, Windows Vista, and Windows 7.
- **Processor**: 1 GHz, recommended: 1.5 GHz or higher.
- **Memory**: 256 MB of RAM minimum, recommended 1 GB or higher.
- **Hard Disk**: 2.0 GB of available space, 10 GB recommended.
- **Video input**: USB 2.0; USB 1.1, FireWire required for digital camcorders.

Any computer that's capable of running Windows Vista and Windows 7 can be used for making movies. It may be possible to use some computers that meet Windows XP's minimum requirements, like netbooks, but we do not recommend this.

A computer with a minimal amount of processing power will run slower and be more difficult to use. Upgrading your computer, or using a better laptop will make your work faster and more enjoyable.

Apple Minimum Requirements

- **Operating System**: Mac OS X 10.4 and later; Mac OS X v10.4.4 required for iMovie themes, real-time effects, and audio effects
- **Processor**: G5 or Intel processor.

- **QuickTime** 7.1 or later
- **Processor:** G5 or Intel core processor.
- **Memory:** 1 GB or more RAM recommended.
- **Hard Disk:** 2.0 GB.
- **Video input:** USB 2.0; USB 1.1, FireWire required for digital camcorders.

Why Free Software?

We make a point of promoting and using free software in this book, in the hopes that someday, if you decide stopmotion is your thing, you'll be able to invest the money saved into better equipment, better software, and better materials to animate. Free software allows you to try before you buy.

Chapter 2

Creating Stories

T-Rex chasing a jeep driven by ninjas! Your first animations will probably be random doodles, lacking any plot or story structure, as you learn the basics of stopmotion; camera angles, frame rates, timing, lighting, set construction, and T-Rex diets.

Eventually, you'll want to start applying these skills towards a more ambitious projects. Animations that tell a story.

As storytellers, animators have an edge over the average *"Hey-d00d! I-got-a-camera-let's-make-a-moveh!!11one!"* guy who grabs people, films them doing stuff, then edits the results together in an afternoon. Instead of a filmmaking style based around constant improvisation, animators are forced to think before they start animating. They visualize the footage needed, then create and animate according to this "mental movie" in their head.

Since any unused, or mis-animated clips represent hundreds of frames of wasted work, the animator is trained to visualize thoroughly and efficiently, a skill both animation and live-action filmmakers should have.

In this chapter, we'll show you how to develop your "mental movies" into easily understandable presentations that can be used to improve your story and share the idea with other people who may be helping with your project.

Writing

You may be dismayed to learn that crafting good movies requires good writing.

Lest you turn to the good ole' excuse: *"I don't need to write anything! It's all in my head!"* there are many reasons why you should get your story on paper in some form before you start animating.

Writing well does not require an English literature major, yet proper grammar, and the ability to form coherent sentences on paper certainly helps.

DISCLAIMER: Stopmotion Explosion is not an English textbook, nor can the author brag about his WGA credentials, or $500k spec script deal. However this chapter will help you formulate your thoughts in a way that will be useful throughout the filmmaking process, and improve the quality of your story.

The Basics

Serious filmmakers start with a written story, called a screenplay. The process of visualizing and planning a film before shooting is called "pre-production." Writing a screenplay is the first part of pre-production.

Short films are great practice for longer projects, and are more likely to be watched in their entirety when posted on video sharing sites, like YouTube.

Writer #1 - "I have no story ideas"

You have writer's block. Here are a bunch of ideas to jump start your right-sided brain.

Adaptation

Adapt a short story, or chapter of a book you like. This could be a couple of paragraphs, a short incident, or "gag" that made you laugh.

Comic Adaptation

Don't read books? Adapt a scene from a comic book. It's already storyboarded.

Movie Adaptation

Find a screenplay for a film that you've never seen, but want to watch. Animate a scene from the screenplay. Then watch the real thing. How does your adaptation measure up to the original? Alternatively, re-make a scene from a video game, or film using stopmotion.

The Joke

Re-tell a dumb joke in movie format. *"Two ropes walk into a..."*

Based on a True Story

Animate something based on a life experience, humorous or otherwise.

School Exercise

Instead of writing a paper for school, present the subject as a short movie (get permission from your teacher first...)

Mashup

Get your storyteller juices flowing by mashing existing stories, characters and places together.

Character #1 goes to **Location** and meets **Character #2**

becomes...

Superman goes to **the supermarket** and meets **Chad Vader**.

Writer #2 - "I have ideas!"

Perhaps you're one of those naturally gifted individuals to whom writer's block is completely unknown *(yeah right)*. Great. Let's start writing!

Sum up your idea in a few short sentences. If you have several ideas, write them all down. You can use pencil and paper, or a computer, whatever feels more natural. If you're not sold on a particular story idea, it may be possible to combine pieces of several ideas into one story. Listing ideas will help you better see what fits together.

After you've outlined the story idea in a paragraph or so, and are happy with the concept, it's time to start working on the screenplay.

The Power of Adjectives

Many stories center around a character with flaws. The character wants something badly, but their desire is impossible to obtain until the flaws in their personality are overcome.

Describing characters with adjectives is a great way to begin defining their personality. We've underlined the adjectives (in bold) describing characters here, along with a goal each character is trying to accomplish.

- "A **shy** politician collects votes"
- "An **angry displaced** beaver builds a dam in his peaceful woodland community"
- "**Dim-witted** secretary transcribes complex reports"
- "**Aquaphobic** life-guard saves baby dolphin"
- "A **loud** drill sergeant takes job as substitute librarian"
- "A **timid** cowboy crosses the Mohave desert... alone"

The personalities of the characters here would make their jobs difficult, even impossible. Strong contrasts between a character's personality and the goal they're trying to accomplish provides plenty of storytelling material.

A hero with a personality that hinders their desires, or hijacks their quest, is a great foundation to build a story on, since the character's journey to achieve their goal is an uphill battle the moment they step out the front door. They become their own worst enemy.

To start, you can ask questions about a character,. Answering these questions will form the framework of your story.

For example, the drill-sergeant-librarian:

- Why is a drill-sergeant working at the library? Is the regular librarian sick?
- Does the librarian greet people loudly when they walk in the door, or are they loud when books are returned late?
- What do the library visitors do when the librarian explodes?
- When does the librarian realize their loudness is hurting their job? Do they change?
- Does a situation arise that allows the librarian to use their loudness for good?
- How does the librarian regain the trust of the patrons?

People you know may provide material for your character's personality. Do you know any loud people? How would they behave if they became a librarian for the day?

Before writing a long screenplay, writers often develop an extended description of the story, called a "treatment" that outlines the entire story, start to finish. Since we're developing a very short film, our paragraph-long description will serve as the treatment. From the treatment, we will write the screenplay.

Properly written screenplays follow a number of formatting and spacing rules. Instead of fussing with margins and type, it's easier to use software that automatically formats your text as you type. We list a few of them at the end of the chapter, and explore the features of Celtx, a free open-source program.

Check it Out!

Here are a couple of pages from the spec-formatted screenplay for *Jack Spelt and the Sandstone Caves*, a short LEGO® film used as an example throughout this book

6.

EXT. GRANDPA SPELT'S HOUSE - NIGHT

                    PIRATE CAPTAIN
          Harr Harr! The map is MINE

The Pirate Captain shoots through the smashed window,
extinguishing the light inside. The world returns to
darkness.

EXT. GRANDPA SPELT'S HOUSE - MORNING

Early morning passerby stare at the kicked-in gate and
window, now shuttered tightly.

INT. GRANDPA SPELT'S HOUSE - MORNING

Grandpa Spelt is seated at his desk. The large painting has
been returned to its place.

                    GRANDPA SPELT
          You must go to the cave and recover
          the treasure before the pirates
          steal it. You are the only living
          descendant and will receive the
          treasure when I die.

Grandpa Spelt wheezes, stressed from the night's ordeal.

JACK SPELT, young, rugged, listens attentively. He scratches
his head.

                    JACK SPELT
          After extensive consideration and
          analysis of the facts available,
          I've concluded my progress will be
          hindered without a map.

                    GRANDPA SPELT
          Precisely my boy, which is why I'm
          giving you this.

Grandpa Spelt reaches under his desk and brings out an MP3
RECORDER.

Jack Spelt rises and stares at the gadget.

                    JACK SPELT
          A digital music player? I've always
          wanted one of those. But.. how on
          earth is it going to help me get
          the treasure?

                                        (CONTINUED)

Jack Spelt Screenplay

```
CONTINUED:                                         7.


                    GRANDPA SPELT
          I've placed an audio tour of the
          sandstone caves on here that will
          guide you to the hiding place of
          the treasure.

He lays the recorder on the table.

                    JACK SPELT
          Umm... OK... if you say so.

                    GRANDPA SPELT
          Good luck my boy.

Jack takes the recorder from the table and EXITS the room.
```

• • • • • • • • • • • • • • • • •

Spec Scripts and Shooting Scripts

Spec scripts are written by enterprising screenwriters hoping to sell their story to a producer. They contain the film's story and dialog, and not much else. Shooting scripts are much more detailed, and are used by the crew and director while the film is in production.

We'll start by creating a screenplay in spec script format, then convert the screenplay into a shooting script.

Use a screenwriting program, like Celtx as you apply the techniques in this section. If you haven't done so already, now would be a good time to download Celtx (link at the end of the chapter) and skim our brief introduction to the program.

Master Scene Format

Screenplays written in Master Scene format are composed of three parts. **Scene Headers**, **Description**, and **Dialog**. One page of screenplay in this format is equal to (roughly) a minute of film. So, a 120 page screenplay is a 120 minute feature film.

All screenplays are written in 12pt Courier font, start with the words FADE IN: and end with FADE OUT.

Scene Headers

Headers or "sluglines" contain three pieces of information:

EXT. CITY STREET - DAY

INT. LIVING ROOM - NIGHT

1. Whether the location is exterior, abbreviated: EXT. or interior, abbreviated: INT.
2. Where the action occurs, for example: BILLY JOE'S GOAT FARM or NEW YORK SUBWAY.
3. What time the action occurs, either: DAY, NIGHT, MORNING, or EVENING.

The last element, time is separated from the first two header elements by spaces and a hyphen. Remember this formula:

EXT. / INT. LOCATION - TIME OF DAY.

You'll need to create a new header each time the location or time changes. For example, if a character inside a subway moves outside, the header needs to change:

INT. NEW YORK SUBWAY - NIGHT

becomes:

EXT. NEW YORK STREET - NIGHT

You can also use LATER, if the location remains the same:

EXT. NEW YORK STREET - LATER

We'll revisit scene headers when we convert our spec script into a shooting script.

Description / Action

The description starts below each scene heading. This is the story within the script, containing actions, visuals, sounds and characters.

Action is always written in the present tense:

`Sally walks to the window`

Past tense is never used:

`Sally walked to the window` **(WRONG!)**

Avoid flowery descriptions. Keep your paragraphs short and sweet. Describe only what is necessary to tell the story.

Write only what can been seen and heard. Emotions, such as *"Fred feels happy"* is non-visual and cannot be seen, but *"Fred smiles"* is a visual emotion that communicates his feelings. Non-visual events, such as thoughts and memories can be shown in flashbacks, dialog, or actions that reveal a character's mind.

Break long paragraphs of action into smaller paragraphs. Starting a new paragraph is a great way to suggest a new camera angle.

Several elements in the action should be written in capitals. This will assist the process of making a shooting script, as the capitalized elements are easier to pick out of the rest of the text. The first two rules are the most important and should always be followed.

- Capitalize all letters of a speaking character's name when they appear for the first time. After this, you may type their name using normal capitalization:

`JOE, 40s, wearing suit and dark shades`

- Capitalize ENTERS and EXITS when used in context of a character entering and exiting a scene:

Joe ENTERS the gas station.

- Capitalize important props and vehicles:

Joe reaches for the SHOVEL

- Capitalize sounds that are essential to telling the story, and will needed to be added afterwards. Example:

Joe sits in the chair. It CREAKS loudly and collapses.

You don't have to capitalize environmental sounds, such as birds chirping, or doors slamming, unless these contribute to the story in some way:

Dialog Blocks

These are the conversations and exclamations of the film. Dialog blocks, sometimes called "speeches" are composed of three parts:

Character Name	BOB
Parentheticals (wrlys)	(to Jordan)
Dialog	More the merrier, I say!

The **character name** is always capitalized.

Parentheticals are also called **wrlys**, due to the poor screenwriting habit of using (wryly) to describe the tone of a character's comment. Parentheticals state how dialog should be said: (loudly), (excitedly) and so forth, when tone isn't immediately apparent from the script.

A script sprinkled with parentheticals usually has poor descriptive text. Actors dislike wrylys, preferring to bring their own interpretation of a role into the dialog. Wrylys should be used is when a group of characters is present, and the writer needs to clarify who the speaker is addressing, (example on the previous page). Otherwise, avoid using parentheticals.

Dialog follows the character name and any parentheticals. If the dialog is offscreen (maybe the character is in another room) the abbreviation (O.S.) is typed after the character's name:

`JOE (O.S.)`
`What came in the mail?`

If a character is narrating in a voice over, the abbreviation (V.O.) is used.

`SGT. FRIDAY (V.O.)`
`I picked the kid up on a 903. Case closed,`
`or so I figured.`

Improving Dialog

Writing dialog that doesn't feel fake is challenging. Much technique can be learned by listening to conversations between real people, paying attention to dialog in films you enjoy, and reading screenplays.

As you write, practice saying your characters' lines out loud. If they sound canned, it's a good indication that something needs to change. Would you say the same thing if you were in their shoes?

Reading your screenplay out loud is a good way to time the length of the movie it will become. (use a stopwatch). If your voice actors are available, you can invite them to read their parts, and adjust for their strengths and weaknesses.

We have passed over some terms and conventions that screenwriters use. We encourage you to learn more through the resources available online, and at your local library.

Celtx

Celtx, the open-source screenwriting program is extremely easy to use. Fire it up (download link at the end of the chapter) and click *Film* in the *Project Templates* splash screen.

The main Celtx window appears. At the bottom of the window, click the *Tile Page* tab.

Fill in the *Title, Author, Copyright* and *Contact Information* fields. If your story is based on an existing work, fill in the *Based On* field too.

Switch back to the *Script* tab. If you look at the upper left corner, you'll see the words *Scene Heading* in a drop-down menu. Click this menu, and select *Text*.

Type FADE IN: all caps. Hit *ENTER* on your keyboard.

Click the drop-down menu again, and click *Scene Heading*, or hit *SHIFT + TAB*. Type out your first scene heading, following the rules we've outlined in this chapter.

Warning!

You are moving into advanced screenwriting territory. These techniques, used during the production of large films, might be overkill for a small project.

Hit the *ENTER* key again, and you'll notice the drop-down menu changes to *Action*. Type in some action, again following the conventions we've outlined in this chapter.

When you're ready to type your first block of dialog, click **Character** in the drop-down menu, or hit **TAB**. Type in the character's name, and hit **ENTER**. The drop-down menu will switch to **Dialog**. Type your dialog lines and hit **ENTER**. Celtx will switch back to **Character**.

- To switch back and forth between **Scene Header** and **Action** mode, hit **SHIFT + TAB**.
- To switch to **Character** and **Dialog** mode, hit **TAB**.

There are several additional modes in the drop-down menu, including **Parentheticals**.

As you type, you'll notice little bars appearing under the text. This is Celtx's autocomplete feature, and it will make your life a lot easier! Hit **ENTER** to insert Celtx's suggestions into your text.

Drafts

After typing FADE OUT. the first draft of the screenplay is complete. Print a few copies and let your friends read it. Ask for their opinion.

Honest opinions can be difficult to find. If your friends think your feelings will be hurt if they criticize something you've written, be vague about the script's authorship.

As a writer, you have to be open to a reader's critique. While criticism may seem like a personal attack, view it as an opportunity to improve your work. Respond correctly. If readers have difficultly understanding a plot element, don't say *"It will make sense in the movie!"* or *"You poor mortals cannot comprehend my genius!"* Revisit the element, introduce it earlier in the script, or cut it out entirely if it doesn't work (often the best choice!) Do whatever it takes to improve your story.

After you've incorporated your readers' input into the screenplay, you've completed the second draft.

And now, it's time to step away. Set the screenplay on a shelf somewhere and forget about it. After a period of self-imposed separation, pick up the screenplay and edit ruthlessly. This is your third draft, and may be the final, if it passes another round of readers with better success than the first draft.

You can continue writing drafts forever. The cycle stops only when you weigh the pros of continued edits against the cons of never shooting the film.

As a new writer/director, you're gaining a wide range of skills, not all of which involve writing. The visual aspects of storytelling are best learned through practical experience. Don't let an endless series of drafts separate you from shooting the film, an experience that will teach you many things which can be applied when you write the next screenplay. There will always be a next time.

Shooting Scripts

After your screenplay has undergone much tweaking, readings, and drafts, you're ready to start shooting. It's time to create a shooting script.

The format of a shooting script allows several people, each playing a different role in the production, to easily extract and organize information relevant to their job. It also allows changes in the script to be tracked and distributed in a way that keeps everyone on the same page. For the lone animator, a shooting script provides a great organizational system for storyboards and video files created during the animation process.

The steps required to create a shooting script are simple.

1. The pages of the screenplay are numbered.
2. The scene headers are numbered.
3. The script is LOCKED and labeled with a Revision Color (White, because it's the first revision... we'll return to this topic)

Locking the Script

Scripts are locked when you're sure no major changes will be made, other people are coming alongside you to assist with the project, and (of course) you're ready to start shooting.

Simply put, locking a script means setting scene and page numbers in stone. They will never change again. Scene 1 will always be Scene 1. Page 6 will always remain Page 6 and so on.

This prevents a lot of confusion. If the director decides to add a couple of pages between the hero's dramatic entrance on Page 6 and the epic duel on Page 7, a change that moves Page 7 to Page 9, everyone's notes about the *"epic duel on Page 7"* will be wrong, resulting in mass panic, wasted work, or worse.

Check it Out!

This is a page from *Jack Spelt and the Sandstone Caves*, after being locked and formatted as a shooting script. See if you can spot the revision, marked with an asterisk (*).

Editing Locked Scripts

New pages, and new scenes are inserted into a script with a letter after the scene or page number.

A scene inserted between 6 and 7 would become scene 6A. Additional scenes would be labeled 6B, 6C and so on.

Pages inserted between page 11 and 12 would become page 11A, 11B, 11C... etc.

Asterisks (*) are placed next to the scene header, and each line of changed text on each changed page. If you compare the locked Jack Spelt script with the unlocked version, you'll notice one of these changes.

Blue Revision - 02-11-09   6.

9   EXT. GRANDPA SPELT'S HOUSE - NIGHT

                        PIRATE CAPTAIN
                Harr Harr! The map is MINE

        The Pirate Captain shoots through the smashed window,
        extinguishing the light inside. The world returns to
        darkness.

10   EXT. GRANDPA SPELT'S HOUSE - MORNING

        Early morning passerby stare at the kicked-in gate and
        window, now shuttered tightly.

11   INT. GRANDPA SPELT'S HOUSE - MORNING

        Grandpa Spelt is seated at his desk. The large painting has
        been returned to its place.

                        GRANDPA SPELT
                You must go to the cave and recover
                the treasure before the pirates
                steal it. You are the only living
                descendant and will receive the
                treasure when I die.

        Grandpa Spelt wheezes, stressed from the night's ordeal.

        JACK SPELT, young, rugged, listens attentively. He scratches
        his head.

                        JACK SPELT
                Without a map, I'm not going to get   *
                very far.

                        GRANDPA SPELT
                Precisely my boy, which is why I'm
                giving you this.

        Grandpa Spelt reaches under his desk and brings out an MP3
        RECORDER.

        Jack Spelt rises and stares at the gadget.

                        JACK SPELT
                A digital music player? I've always
                wanted one of those. But.. how on
                earth is it going to help me get
                the treasure?

(CONTINUED)

Jack Spelt Shooting Screenplay

Finally, the revision color and date of the revision is placed in the header of every page.

If a scene is removed from the script, the header and action is deleted, and OMITTED is written next to the scene number:

68   OMITTED

Revision Colors

A new color revision is issued every time the locked script is changed. Instead of numbered revisions, such as "Revision 1.0," followed by "Revision 2.0," the first "White Revision" is followed by the "Blue Revision." The colors progress in this order:

- White
- Blue
- Pink
- Yellow
- Green
- Goldenrod
- Buff
- Salmon
- Cherry
- Tan
- Gray
- Ivory

Since revisions change a few pages at most, the pages with changes are printed in the color of the revision, and inserted into scripts, which are kept in three-ring binders for this reason.

See how this works? Following proper locked-script procedure prevents the necessity of printing a new script every time something changes.

Here's a step-by-step guide to locking a screenplay in Celtx, and creating a shooting script.

What If?

If all the colors in the list are used (it does happen!) the entire script is reprinted in blue. Any changes to this "double-blue" revision are printed in "double-pink" and the whole cycle of colors begins again.

White Revision

At the top of the screen, click **Script > Revision Mode...** The **Revision Options** window will appear. Check **"Lock Scenes."** Rename **"Revision 1"** to **"White Revision"** followed by the date. **"White Revision - mm/dd/ yyyy."** Finally, click the **Revision Color** drop-down menu and change **"Blue"** to **"White."**

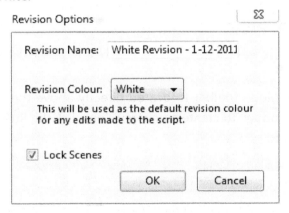

Click the **Type/Set** tab at the bottom of the screen to preview the results. The title page should have the revision name and date under the script title, and all the scenes and pages in your script should be numbered. That was pretty easy!

If you don't see scene numbers, click the **Format Options** button, and in the **Show scene numbers** drop-down menu, change **None** to **Left**.

Do a *"Save As..."* and save your locked Celtx file with the revision color and date in the filename.

Unfortunately, revisions are the Achilles heel of Celtx. As of this writing, Celtx lacks the ability to:

1. Properly label revised pages with the revision color. Celtx renames every page in the shooting script with the new revision color, instead of just the pages changed, as is typically done.

2. You cannot export only the pages changed by a revision. For example, if the Blue revision has changed three pages of the White revision, and you want to send your friends the three new Blue pages and a Blue title page to insert into their White scripts. Celtx will not export these individual pages. Currently, Celtx only exports PDFs of the entire script.

This said, there is a slightly wonky workaround to these two problems.

Blue Revision

The Revision Mode toolbar is located directly above the script in the main Celtx window. To create a new revision, click the little green plus icon on the left.

As when creating the White revision, rename *"Revision 1"* to *"Blue Revision"* followed by the date. *"Blue Revision - mm/dd/yyyy."* Finally, click the *Revision Color* drop-down menu and change *"White"* to *"Blue."*

Make your changes to the script. This is the Blue Revision. Do a *"Save As...,"* and create a new Celtx file with the draft color and date in the filename:

MyGreatScreenplay_BLUE-01-23-2011.celtx

This will ensure the Blue revision is saved, and the White revision is preserved as a separate file.

Exporting Blue Pages

Export the entire Blue revision as a PDF, with the draft color and date in the PDF's filename:

MyGreatScreenplay_BLUE-01-23-2011.pdf

Using a PDF reader's *"Print Range"* feature (Adobe Reader, or equivalent) print only the title page and the pages changed in the blue revision, make copies with colored paper and a photocopier, and insert the pages into White revision scripts. Tada! Blue revision scripts!

Alternatively, you can print the Blue pages (on white paper) scan them into a PDF, and email them to your fellow animators, allowing them to print their own copies.

The absence of a proper revisions feature in Celtx can be a huge hassle, (especially when you start approaching the Cherry revision) but if you are working by yourself, or with a few additional people, revisions aren't as critical as they become on larger projects. If you're a serious filmmaker and thinking about writing your first feature film, or starting a project with a crew larger than five people, switch to commercial software, such as Final Draft.

Robin Hood Storyboard

Storyboarding

Storyboards are a lot like comic strips. Blank storyboards are sheets of paper covered with little squares. The movie is drawn into the squares shot by shot. Usually a few lines are written under the square describing what happens in the shot.

The storyboard helps you plan camera angles, character movement, set design, character design, prop placement, camera movement, all the visual elements of your film.

You may be thinking: *"I can't draw so I can't make a storyboard."* If you can draw a stick figure with a nose, you can make a storyboard. Use the noses to show which way a figure is facing. That's it!

Typically, storyboards are drawn from the script, though it is possible to draw an entire film in storyboard format. If you can't be troubled to scribble out a script, at least take time to storyboard.

Each square in the storyboard should be labeled with the scene number from the script, and a second number, the "shot number." The first storyboard square of the scene is **shot 1**, the second square is **shot 2**, and so on. If two squares are used to illustrate the same shot, they should be lettered: **Shot 2A** and **Shot 2B**.

Storyboards help you to visualize your movie before animating. This will assist you in cutting out unnecessary visuals that make movies slow and boring, instead of quick and snappy.

Screenplays and storyboard are tools for communicating with others. The only way your fellow animators will see the story in your head is through scripts and storyboards.

Screenwriting Software for Pros

Final Draft. Many options for formatting and viewing your screenplay. Currently priced around $250.

Movie Magic Screenwriter. Comes with several templates and screenplay examples. Priced comparatively to Final Draft, about $250. Company has been noted for great customer service. Academic pricing is available for both Final Draft and Movie Magic.

> **www.finaldraft.com**
> **www.screenplay.com**

Free Software

If investing hundreds of dollars in screenwriting software isn't your cup of tea, you may be interested in the many free options available. *Celtx* is a free program that contains many features of the programs above. Be sure to watch the many instructional videos on the Celtx website!

> *www.celtx.com*

Online Tools

Zhura and *Plotbot.* Online screenwriting tools are fabulous if you are working on a project with several people, and all of them need to access the script at once. Both of these services are free, as of this writing.

> *www.zhura.com*
> *www.plotbot.com*

Chapter 3

Building Sets

Sets are the world your characters inhabit as they move through events in your story. Stopmotion sets can be very simple. The story may take place on an arctic ice flo, which could be made from a white tabletop and blue paper sky. Or, the story could take place in a dusty western town, made of tan construction paper, storefronts constructed from LEGO® bricks and distant mountains made from torn posterboard.

Building Materials

Here's a bunch of stuff around the house that could be used in your set. Acquire a new eye for everyday objects. "What would this look like if I was three inches tall?"

Towel

Green: Grass, distant mountain, fuzzy slime monster.
Blue: Gigantic tidal wave, bottom of mysterious ocean cave, deep shag carpet.

Rug

Grab pillows, blocks, books and other bulky objects. Shove under rug to create instant hilly terrain.

Paper

Crumpled paper: Bush, tree, iceberg, boulder, termite mound, giant meteor.
Flat paper: Ground, sky, distant horizon, ice, water, road sign.

Cardboard box

Buildings, skyscrapers, apartments, shack, spaceship, boat, cliff walls. Dress up with more cardboard, make drawings, cut holes in the sides with a serrated knife, think of the box as a "base" to bulk up with other materials.

Packaging Stuff

Found in the boxes of new printers and computers. Ancient temple walls. The surface of a futuristic spacecraft. A hydroelectric dam.

Wire

Jungle vines, plumbing, iron rebar, rope.

Drinking straw

Steam pipes, flying saucer legs, smokestack, bazooka.

Ball of clay

Beanbag chair, TV set, fire hydrant... mold it into anything you want!

Additionally, you can animate inside the playsets created for some action figures, use models from any LEGO® set, Playmobile® buildings, Lincoln Logs™, K'NEX®, nearly any construction themed toy can be used for set building.

If you wish to build more complex sets, reading about diorama building, model railway construction, and dollhouse interior design will teach you more about the art of building in miniature.

Designing Sets

Before you start building, pull out your storyboards and study them. Look at all the different locations your characters visit, and the camera angles you have planned for each shot. When you finish, you'll know the number of sets to build, and how they should be designed. This is called "breaking down" a script. In this example, you're making a specific kind of breakdown, called a "location breakdown." If you listed all the props in the script, you would have a "prop breakdown." A list of all the vehicles would be called a "vehicle breakdown" and so on.

When designing the set, it's helpful to ask yourself two questions:

1. Where will the camera go?
2. Where will my fingers go?

Indoor Sets

Interior sets can be built with one wall, two walls, or three. You'll want to leave at least one wall of the set open so the camera can see inside.

You can build sets with four walls, but make the walls easy to remove from the structure. If you need a different camera angle, you'll be able to pull the wall off the set and shoot from there.

The number of walls required depends on the camera angles you'll be using, and this can be quickly be determined by looking over your storyboards. (We told you storyboards were important!)

The walls should be tall enough so you can't see behind the set.

This set was used in the film *Jack Spelt and the Sandstone Caves*. The interior shots showed only the door, and the corner of the room, so just two walls had to be built, leaving the rest of the set open for animating work.

In the second set, we had shots of characters sitting on both sides of the room, so we built a set with three walls, and a hallway on the side.

Notice these sets do not have ceilings. Stopmotion sets with ceilings are a bad idea. They make it impossible to light the set properly, (your lighting is typically placed above the set), and difficult to move objects as you animate.

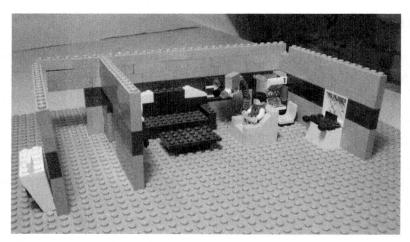

If you can see through windows in your set, create some sky by placing some blue paper outside the window. You can also use objects that look like buildings, animate cars driving by, anything to enhance the illusion that your set is located in a "real" world, surrounded by a dynamic, changing environment!

Outdoor Sets

It's important to have a nice backdrop. A big piece of sky-blue paper placed behind the set is a great starting place. It's easy to cut a few hills out of green paper, or the outlines of a few buildings and tape them

to the "sky." Some office and art supply stores sell sheets of posterboard with printed clouds.

Green posterboard is an excellent "grass" surface. You can also use green LEGO® baseplates, fabric, and other materials.

Another useful set-building material is a foamcore folding

panel that's typically used for displays at science fairs. It stands up by itself, and can surround a small set.

If you have certain kinds of action, like a car on the road or a flying plane, you can keep the object in one place and move the background instead of the car. This is technique is similar to the "looping backgrounds" seen in many cartoons.

City Sets

The simplest way to make buildings for your stop motion city? Build false fronts with nothing behind them. If you construct a bunch of these fake buildings and set them up in a row, they look great!

If your building materials are limited, pull out your storyboards and set breakdown. Pick out all the shots that take place on one set. Build the set, capture all the shots, then pull the set apart and build it into something new. If you're creating a LEGO® movie with a small collection of bricks, you can reuse them over and over again. It's time-consuming to

move back and forth between two sets. If possible, animate all the footage you need at a set in one go, then move to the next set.

Securing Your Sets

Imagine you're animating a very exciting part of your movie:

Flying Fennris, skateboarder, is burning up the pavement. He swerves around a light pole. He grinds down a handrail. Suddenly the ground starts shaking back and forth. Fennris isn't fazed. He continues swerving between pedestrians like gravity is out of style. Despite his entire world moving every few frames, he doesn't feel it!

You probably forgot to fasten your set to the table. Adjusting a character or object between frames is enough to nudge the set out of alignment. Also, don't rule out the possibility of bumps and knocks from your own elbows and sleeves!

Ooops...

This animation setup is a simple plywood table built into a corner of a closet. The wire shelf above the set is convenient for storing supplies and hanging lights.

Stick the set to your table with double sided tape, or hold it down with c-clamps and heavy books.

Another way to lessen noticeable bumps is to attach your camera to the set itself. When you move your set accidentally, the camera moves with the set and the movement isn't as noticeable. You'll need a large base for the set, and you'll still need to be sure the lighting stays in the right places.

Chapter 4

Cameras

To create stopmotion films, you'll need a camera that sends a video image to your computer. If you're a beginner, you'll want a camera that is small, easy to use, and inexpensive.

All of these qualities are found in the webcam, a small USB camera used for video chatting over the Internet. Webcams offer the most bang for the animator's buck!

You can also use camcorders and digital still cameras for animating. If you are looking for the best possible image quality, use a digital camcorder, or digital still camera. These cameras are explained at the end of this chapter.

The price of a good webcams continues to drop, but manufacturers are accomplishing this by discarding features necessary for creating high-quality animations. There are several features you'll want to look for.

Choosing a Camera

Manual controls. Many cheaper cameras have "fixed focus" and automatically adjust the camera settings for changes in the camera's environment. Automatic controls are great if you're using a webcam to chat with friends or film a video blog post, but they cause problems for animators. Often you can find the camera's instruction booklet online, or reviews of the camera's features. Make sure you can adjust the camera's focus, exposure, and white balance manually.

You should be able to focus on objects that are very close to the camera lens – 1½ inches (3 cm) if possible. This will give you greater creativity and freedom with the camera angles you choose for your film.

The bigger your camera sensor is, the sharper and clearer the image created will be. It's common to find cameras with 1.3 **MP**, or **Megapixels**. These are great for animating.

Many webcams are designed for use with laptop computers. These have a small clip or "hinge" on the bottom of the camera for mounting on top of the laptop's screen. If you can read the camera's manual, or there are pictures on the camera's box, make sure you can bend the hinge, or remove the clip in a way that allows you to set the camera on a flat surface, like a table.

It's common to find small cameras embedded in laptops and the latest Apple and Dell desktops. These cameras can be used for animating, if you're animating a drawing on a whiteboard, people, large stuffed animals, etc.

Some cameras also have a threaded hole, allowing the camera to be mounted on a tripod. This is a nice extra.

Camera Words

Pixel: The camera sensor converts an image into thousands of tiny colored dots, called pixels.

Sensor: An electronic chip that converts light into numbers, telling the computer the brightness and color that a picture contains. There are two types of sensors: CCD and CMOS. A webcam sensor might have "300K" pixels, meaning 300,000. A digital still camera might have "3 Megapixels," or 3 million pixels.

CCD: A type of sensor used in some webcams. Webcams with these sensors are uncommon. Typically, they cost more.

CMOS: A type of sensor used in most newer webcams.

Resolution: The number of pixels an image contains. The more pixels a picture has, the better quality it will be. A 640 x 480 image is 640 pixels wide and 480 high (a good resolution for simple stopmotion work).

Auto Exposure: Most webcams have software that automatically adjusts the exposure to keep the picture well lit. When you're animating, you'll want to turn off this feature and set the exposure yourself.

Mac and Windows Webcams

To date, webcams have had the most support on Windows-based computers. This is changing as Macs increase in popularity, and new webcam drivers are written.

While most cameras come with Windows drivers and software, you may have to visit the manufacturer's website for an Mac driver, or use a driver created by a third party.

The **Macam** community has banded together and created a free collection of webcam drivers for OS X. They also maintain a giant list of mac-compatible cameras on the Macam website. If your camera is supported and on the list, you can download and install the free OS X driver.

If you're uncertain whether your camera is supported, check the list of webcams here:

http://webcam-osx.sourceforge.net/

The list of supported cameras is continuously growing, and support for existing cameras continue to be improved, so check back often!

Webcams that conform to the **UVC (USB Video Class)** are compatible with OS X 4.3 and all later versions, as well as Windows XP, Windows Vista and Windows 7.

Logitech

Logitech has made many webcams that are very suitable for animating. The **Logitech Quickcam 4000** is dated, but still an excellent choice for Mac and Windows animators. The **Quickcam 9000** and **Logitech Quickcam Vision Pro** are also worth a look.

Apple iSight

There are two versions of the **iSight** camera. The internal version is placed in iMac and iBook screens. The external version plugs into your computer's FireWire port. The external iSight is not recommended because the image controls are difficult to adjust, and it's rather large. There are scattered reports of the camera working on Windows-based computers, but no official driver exists.

Philips SPC900NC

The camera has a small, white LED that may need to be covered with tape to prevent unwanted shadows. Image quality is good, and the camera's base can be adjusted to sit flat on a table.

If you shop around, it's possible to purchase a used webcam for around $20-40 bucks. Check out eBay.

Camera Image Controls

You will encounter these controls in the menus of nearly any camera you use. Don't be afraid to grab knobs and sliders and tweak them until you understand what they do. This is a camera, not the control room of a nuclear power plant!

Brightness: The eye's perception of light in an image. Cameras that let you control brightness do so by adding light to all the colors in the image.

Contrast: The eye's perception of difference in brightness or color between details of a picture that are next to each other. Adjusting contrast takes light away from dimmer areas and adds more light to the brighter areas of a picture.

Gain: An electronic enhancement that affects brightness. Increasing the gain makes dimly lit areas seem brighter without changing the exposure. This can produce "noise" or graininess in the picture.

Gamma: Refers to an electronic correction that is used to keep colors looking natural on different media such as computer monitors, photo prints, and color printers.

Hue: Changes the way the camera "sees" color. If you want to adjust the color of your image, you're better off adjusting the white balance.

Saturation: Controls the amount of color in an image. A highly saturated image has lots of color. Low saturation produces a black-and-white image.

Exposure: The amount of time the camera allows light to fall on the electronic sensor. The higher the exposure level is set, the brighter the picture will be—but if set too high, the picture will look washed out. Also called "shutter speed."

Flicker: Settings compensate for flicker created by fluorescent lighting. Cameras are sensitive to this. In the US use the "60Hz" setting.

White Balance: Adds color to the image until white objects appear white. In the camera, ordinary light bulbs will appear "warmer" and reddish, while fluorescents and sunlight will appear "cooler" and blue.

Using a Webcam

As soon as you get your webcam out of its packaging, follow the manufacturer's installation instructions.

To test the camera, start up your stopmotion software.

A live picture should appear in the software's video window.

A webcam plugged into a computer's USB port

If the image is blurry, twist the focus ring encircling the lens until the picture is clear.

If your camera doesn't have manual focus (a focus ring,) you can

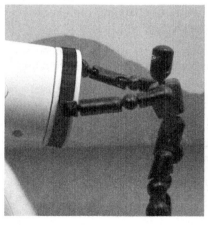

use the camera for basic animation purposes, but it's fairly useless. You won't be able to capture the close up images that really bring stopmotion to life.

Your camera is set up and ready to use. If you have enough light and the picture looks decent, you could move onto the next chapter and try a little animating. If you want to keep tweaking the camera settings for the best image possible, read the next section.

Camera Controls

Taking time to master your camera's image controls will improve the visual impact of your productions.

Your stopmotion software should have an option on the menu

called *Camera Controls, Camera Options, Source* or something similar. This screenshot shows where to find the camera settings in SMA.

Laptops with internal webcams are becoming more common. In these situations you'll need to select the camera you're using to animate in the animation software. In SMA, click *Options > Source > Capture Source.*

The camera menu pictured may differ from the menu for your camera, but you'll find the same basic image controls in the software for most webcameras.

Have your set well lit and the webcam in place before starting these adjustments.

Exposure

In SMA, click *Options* then *Source*. In the *Settings* tab, uncheck the *Auto* box next to the *Exposure* slider. Adjusting the camera's exposure changes the brightness of the image. If the exposure is allowed to automatically adjust itself, flickers and changes in image

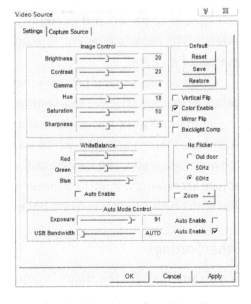

brightness may appear. For example, if your hand reaches into the set to move something, the automatic exposure will kick in, and the camera image will become brighter. The adjustment takes a few seconds, and you may grab a frame before the picture returns to its original state.

This brighter frame will be visible in the completed footage, creating an unwanted flicker effect.

After turning off automatic exposure, you will need to set the exposure to a desirable level. Move the exposure slider until the picture is bright again.

White Balance

White balance allows you to compensate for different colors of light by changing the color of white in an image.

Let's explain this. If you're inside reading this book next to a lamp, the light shining on the pages is yellow. The camera sees the yellowish light and compensates by adjusting the image color until the lamp appears white.

White balance is set by placing the camera in front of a white object, like a piece of paper, and pushing or clicking a button that "sets" the balance. The camera tweaks the image, adjusting the colored light until the paper is white.

Cameras are usually pretty good at automatically adjusting white balance, so you can leave this setting at auto.

To manually set the white balance on your camera, uncheck the auto box. Place a sheet of white paper in front of the camera. Check the auto box again. The camera will sample the white of the paper and adjust accordingly. If you continue animating with the same lighting, you won't have to set the white balance again.

Other Settings

Some cameras have the ability to adjust for flicker created by fluorescent lights. If your camera has anti-flicker controls, try setting them to 50 or 60Hz.

Other settings, like brightness and contrast are fairly self-explanatory. Take a few moments to play with the sliders and watch their effect on the image.

In addition to the image controls mentioned here, some cameras have an autofocus setting. This is found in digital video cameras, and some higher-end webcams. If possible, turn the autofocus control off, and adjust the focus manually.

Using Camcorders

If you own a camcorder, you have access to some nice features.

- Real optical zoom, not a "fake" digital zoom, which is simply the camera doubling the size of the image and discarding the edges of the frame, making everything seem closer.
- Greater image control, more settings to tweak, and better low-light performance.

All this production-enhancing goodness could be featured in your next film if you had a way to connect the camera to your computer. How do you do this?

Digital Camcorders

Digital camcorders output video through FireWire connectors.

This is what a FireWire port on the computer looks like. Sometimes you'll see the number "1394," sometimes you'll see a FireWire symbol. These ports come in 6 and 4-pin versions.

4-pin FireWire port

6-pin FireWire port

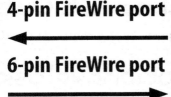

This is what a FireWire cable looks like. Notice the large and small ends. Typically, the larger 6-pin connector plugs into the computer, the small 4-pin connector plugs into the camera.

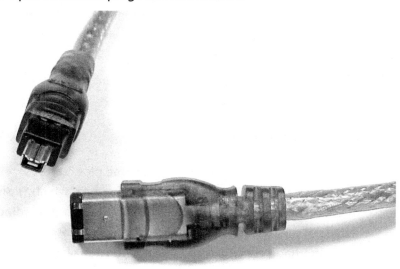

It's common for laptop computers to have a small 4-pin FireWire port instead of the larger 6-pin style. You can purchase adapters that will convert a large 6-pin FireWire cable into the smaller four-pin version. These are very handy.

Once the computer and camera are connected, you can use the camcorder like an ordinary webcam.

By using your camera's zoom, you should be able to get good closeups even if the camera is too big to fit into your set.

Check It Out!

A special driver is required to use camcorders with the SMA animation program. This driver can be downloaded from:

StopmotionExplosion.com

Note, whether you're using an analog or digital camera, you'll need to make all adjustments and changes to the camera controls through the camera's menus, buttons and switches.

Many camcorders have an autofocus setting that should be disabled, otherwise the camera will constantly be focusing on your fingers as you move them in and out of the set. Auto exposure should also be disabled.

Use your camera's AC adapter and plug into a power outlet, otherwise you'll run out of battery power long before your animating session is over.

Digital Still Cameras

Stopmotion does not necessarily require a camera that's capable of capturing video. You're capturing one frame at a time, so normal still cameras can be used.

A digital still camera, capturing images with 10+ million pixels offers the ultimate in video resolution, making it the camera of choice for high-end stopmotion films.

In-Camera Animation

Many people are already using a digital still camera to animate. They take pictures of their characters moving, one picture at a time, and "play" the pictures by quickly scrolling through them with the camera's preview button. This is a simple way to make animations with a point-'n-shoot, or DSLR, but you can do better!

Camera Design

Most stopmotion software functions by grabbing frames from a live video source. Most low-end still cameras will not send video to the computer, even when the two are connected by a USB cable. Even if you are sending video to the computer, it won't be sent at the camera's full resolution. And that beautiful resolution is why we're going through all this trouble in the first place!

If you MUST get video output from a still camera, you're more likely to find a VIDEO OUT through RCA jacks or HDMI. Some cameras have this option, so check the manual. Again, you won't be getting the camera's full resolution.

DSLRs

Many DSLRs, such as those sold by Nikon and Canon output a "live view" from the camera over USB. Additionally, you can purchase stopmotion programs, such as **Dragon Stopmotion**, sold by **DZED Systems** that interface with the camera, via USB.

How do you animate with a still camera without live view?

Here's one way to accomplish this. The digital camera is pointed at the set, and plugged into the wall, (to avoid the all-to common problem of batteries draining in the middle of the shoot).

A webcam is pointing at the camera's little preview screen. The webcam is plugged into a computer running SMA, or your favorite stopmotion software.

Basically, every time you move something, you're clicking two buttons. Every time you take a picture with the still camera, you grab a frame in SMA. This creates a low-resolution preview of your work in SMA. You can discard the preview when you're done. The real frames of the animation remain on the camera's memory card.

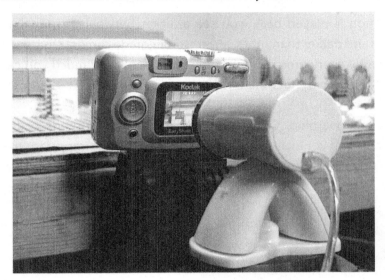

Frame Conversion

When you're finished animating with your still camera, you've created hundreds and hundreds of picture files that need to be converted into a single video file, or several video files, depending on the number of scenes you're animated.

Some people will bring these frames into a video editing program, like **Windows Movie Maker**. The editor strings the frames together, and plays them back slowly. It's a semi-passible way to make a stopmotion movie. You can do better!

In this book, you'll find instructions for a useful program called **VirtualDub**. With VirtualDub, it's easy to convert a series of pictures into video. You'll find a detailed explanation of the process in the VirtualDub chapter.

Other Considerations...

Make sure the camera is fastened down tightly while snapping frames. If your camera can use a remote shutter release, it wouldn't be a bad idea to purchase one. You want to touch the camera little as possible.

Most low-end cameras suffer from a flicker problem. When the animation is played back, you see a flicker between frames that are lighter and darker than others. A consumer grade camera shutter closes differently every time you take a picture. There's not much you can do about this, besides getting a higher quality camera. DSLR setups work best.

A final warning. Capturing thousands and thousands of frames may damage your camera shutter. If your camera is important to you, don't risk it on stopmotion films!

Camera Stabilization

There are many shapes and sizes of webcams. Nearly every design has a few weaknesses that can be mended with a strategic application of high-tech bonding materials. Pieces of tape, in other words.

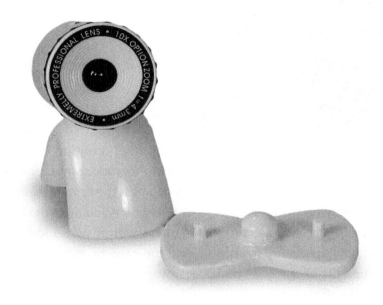

Let's customize this camera for stopmotion usage with a few simple modifications.

A nice feature of this webcam is the detachable mounting plate. The threaded hole in the bottom of the plate fits a standard tripod screw.

The black ring behind the lens is the *focus ring*. Twist it to the left to focus on far-away things. Twist it right to focus on close-up objects. (Try focusing on your fingers and examining the dirt on your fingertips).

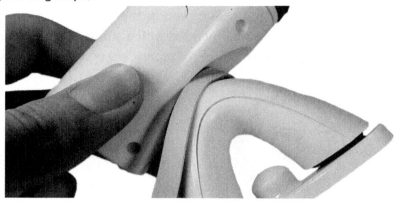

Many webcams, this camera included, have a button on top that lets you grab single frames and save them to your computer. Making animations this way is <u>not</u> recommended, unless the camera is *extremely* stable. Otherwise the image will jump every time you push the button.

This camera is connected to the stand with a swivel joint. While swivel joints are handy for positioning the camera, they're usually at fault when the image goes bump. Just wiggling the cord often swivels the camera off target.

Fortunately, there's a simple solution. Rubber bands!

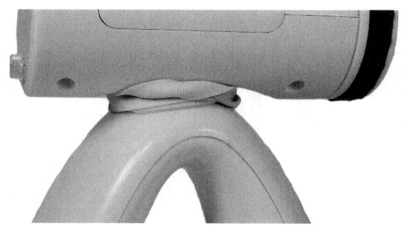

Wrap a rubber band tightly between the camera and stand. Your goal is to immobilize this joint, making it stiffer. (We used two rubber bands on this camera. You'll need more if yours aren't very thick).

Done! Grab some tape for the next step.

We used black electrical tape, because it's sticky, easy to cut, and doesn't leave a residue on the camera. Also, black tape *just looks cool*, but any tape should work fine.

Start wrapping the tape around the camera and stand. Removing the tripod plate makes this job easier.

Aside, if you want to keep the camera's swivel feature, this step should be skipped. If you continue wrapping, you'll lose the ability to swivel the camera back and forth, but the camera will have maximum stability.

Webcams can be customized in many different ways, depending on the animator's needs.

This super-taped and rubber-banded camera was spotted on the set of *Jack Spelt and the Sandstone Caves*. Someone added a roll of tape to the bottom of the camera for extra weight.

Links

Dragon Stopmotion
http://www.dragonstopmotion.com/

The webcam above has been attached to a LEGO® plate. Fastening the camera to a set is easy! Below, we have another LEGO® webcam stand, this one using a round camera.

Chapter 5

Lighting

Good lighting is key to creating a visually dynamic picture.

Bad Lights

A couple of light sources should be ruled out immediately.

Light fixtures on the ceiling aren't bright enough and light falling over your shoulder onto the set will create shadows. You need to bring the light to your set.

The sun moves, and clouds keep passing overhead, creating shadows. Animating in the sun would require working quickly, on a perfect day. Who wants to animate indoors when the sun is shining outside?

Good Lights

A few desk lamps, clip lights, or a mix of both provide plenty of light. Lights are especially useful if they have clamps or clips of some kind, allowing them to be placed creatively during setup, and secured tightly during filming.

Preferably, your animation setup should be lit with two or three lights.

Three Point Lighting

Using the basic "three-point" lighting technique, lights are placed on the left and right sides of a subject. A third light is directed at the subject from behind. This creates a edge of light on the subject's shoulders and hair, helping to separate them from the background. A fourth light (if needed) is used to light the background.

If your sets and figures are small, you can easily light your animation setup with two light sources (say two desk lamps). Place one lamp on the right side of the set, and the other on the left. Boom! You're done.

Three-Point Lighting

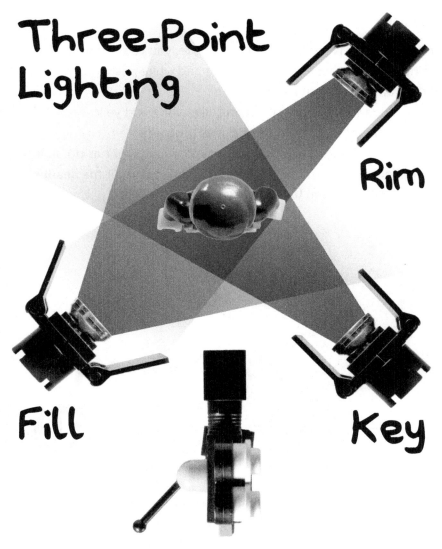

Rim

Fill

Key

A bright focused light is placed on one side of the subject. This light is called the **Key**. The **Fill**, a softer, diffused light is placed on the opposite side, filling in shadows created by the Key. A Fill light doesn't have to be pointed directly at the subject, it can be bounced off walls and flat, light-colored surfaces. The **Rim** light is pointed at the subject from behind, separating the subject from the background.

Tweaking

If your lighting is too bright, causing glare, you can soften the light by pointing your light sources at the walls and white poster board. This will diffuse and spread out it out.

Wear dark clothing. Light colors, like white and yellow reflect light back on the set, which can cause flicker problems

You'll also want to block out as much natural light as possible and avoid light sources placed behind you. Pull down all the shades and shut off every lamp in the room except your set lights.

The clip lamp pictured here uses a compact fluorescent bulb. These bulbs use less electricity, and stay cooler than regular lightbulbs. CFLs also come in "floodlight" versions that throw a lot of light out.

Use caution when animating with desk lamps! Use bulbs with the recommended wattage, and be careful... they get hot! Turn your lights off when you leave the room.

Does the video you create flicker, even though you've carefully controlled the lighting? The camera's auto exposure setting may be turned on. Auto exposure monitors the light falling on the camera's sensor. If the light changes, for example, your hand moves in front of the camera for a moment, auto exposure compensates by changing the camera settings.

Your stopmotion software may have an option in one menu labeled *Camera controls*, *Camera options* or something similar. It will display a window with several controls that modify the camera's image, the color, brightness, saturation, exposure, and so on.

If *Exposure* is set to *Auto*, uncheck the box, or check *Manual*. *Exposure Lock* might be another label for this setting.

If you are animating with a camcorder attached to the animation software, you will have to change this setting in the camera menus. Consult your camera's instruction book.

Now, when you put your hand in front of the camera, the lighting won't be affected. When you take your hand away, the picture will remain the same.

Keep moving your lights around until your scenes are lit correctly

Lighting Effects

Flashlights are handy for mood lighting. Think of them as little spotlights.

If your flashlight is bright and focused, it will create a small spot of glare in the camera's image.

This glare can be an explosion, arc-welding flare, rocket lift-off, transporter beam, or whatever the story needs. Enhance the effect by moving the flashlight slightly in each frame.

By wrapping colored plastic wrap or tissue paper over a flashlight, the light can be red, orange, yellow, (good fire colors) or green and blue (space, night effects).

A big desk lamp can be moved into many positions. If you're trying to create outdoor lighting, it can be raised and lowered to cast shadows for any hour of the day.

Fire

Scraps of colored plastic, or small transparent red, yellow and orange

LEGO® bricks are a great fire "base." Use a flashlight pointing down on the flames for some glow.

The red dot of a laser pointer looks "grainy" when you capture it with a webcam. These grains (or dots) can achieve the illusion of leaping flames. If you shine the pointer at a transparent plastic object, it creates a glowing light effect. Laser "fires" look best with very little extra lighting. The laser beam will wash out in a brightly lit scene.

Never look directly at a laser pointer's beam! Kids, ask permission before using one.

Indoor Lighting

Putting a flashlight inside a set creates a warm glow.

You can enhance the glow by taping paper, or small pieces of masking tape across the inside of the windows. These coverings will catch and diffuse the light, making it easier to see.

Lightning

1. Turn off all your set lights except one. Move it back far enough so the set is fairly dark.
2. Start rapidly clicking the capture button.
3. Quickly swing the light towards the set, and away from the set. You'll see the frames of your animation brighten and darken.
4. Play back the frames you have captured. This effect may require some experimentation to get the best results.
5. Add thunderclap sound effects.

Chapter 6

Composition

Starry Night *by Vincent van Gogh.*

Composition is the art of arranging elements within a picture in such a way that the image is balanced and pleasing to the eye.

If you look at a picture and squint, the tiny details disappear, and you see a collection of lines, shapes, and colors. The arrangement of these elements pull the eye towards certain areas, and away from others.

Composition is an important storytelling tool. Filmmakers want the audience to concentrate on specific details during the progression of their film, and composition is a means by which this is accomplished.

Mesquite Mike does not like Panhandle Pete. Mike is a big, tall bully.

Here's an example. Say we want to film a showdown between the town bully and a little cowpoke. To emphasize the large, imposing bully, we film him from below, looking upward.

To emphasize the insignificance of the cowpoke, we film him from an upper angle, as if we were the bully looking down on the brim of his hat.

Panhandle Pete is surprised to see Mesquite Mike. Pete is a short cowpoke

As you plan the composition of your shots, choose angles that tell the story of your movie.

Rule of Thirds

Dividing an image into halves should be avoided. This is called "bisecting." Nature is rarely bisected. Instead we find collections of objects clumped into harmonious balance. We can avoid bisecting by applying the Rule of Thirds.

To apply this rule, mentally divide your image into a perfect tic-tac-toe grid with four intersecting lines. Place areas of interest so they fall under or around the four points.

Look at the image of a man and his motorcycle. The character is underneath the left line with his face almost beneath the top left cross. The motorcycle is underneath the lower right cross and bottom horizontal line.

Rule of Thirds grid. Important areas under the crosses.

As a rule of thumb, keep important things out of the middle of the squares and under the lines. This will ensure your shot is composed correctly.

Lines and Triangles

When framing and composing your shots, always remember "less is more." The most brilliant compositions are not the most cluttered, but those that draw attention to essential areas, and tell a story with them.

Triangle Rule

Important objects in an image should be arranged in such a way that they form a triangle. The viewer follows the lines of this triangle, until the eye has visited every area of the image.

In this picture, you can see how a triangle is formed by the character's face, the door of the house, and the motorcycle wheel.

Lines of Composition

Lines in your image also form triangles, which emphasize certain areas.

See how the lines created by the top and bottom of the house point towards the character's face? Additional lines along the bottom of the image point towards the motorcycle. Finally, the character forms a triangle, which again draws the eye towards his face.

Composition can be learned by studying art and images around you. As an exercise, try tracing triangles of composition in a magazine or newspaper ad.

Selective Focus

Focus on the foreground character

Hold your finger close to your eye and look at it. Notice how everything behind your finger blurs out? Achieving this effect with a camera is called selective focus, or Depth of Field (DOF). If an image has "deep" DOF, everything in the image will appear sharply in focus. If an image

Focus on the background character

has "shallow" DOF, a small part of the image will be in focus. These two images have a very shallow DOF.

Shallow DOF allows the camera and audience to focus on specific areas of an image, in this case, drawing attention to characters in the foreground and background. Deep DOF shows all areas of the image at once.

Frames and Composition

You may have heard of "widescreen" and "standard" video. These terms refer to the shape of the video frame. The shape of the frame will change the image's composition.

An "aspect ratio" is two numbers, the ratio of the long side of a shape to the short side of a shape.

For example, the aspect ratio of a 4-by-3 rectangle is 4:3. This is the aspect ratio of a standard video frame. Most webcams have a standard frame.

Widescreen video has an aspect ratio of 16:9. Some webcams, and all HD cameras shoot widescreen video.

The flat rectangular shape of a widescreen frame offers more creative composition possibilities than the square 4:3 frame.

For example, the composition of the 4:3 image on the next page is so-so. Key elements are placed under the thirds grid, but there's a lot of blank space at the top and bottom of the frame.

Now the frame is cropped to the bottom 16:9 image, the thirds grid has changed, and the composition looks a lot better.

The rules of composition can be broken for storytelling effect. If a filmmaker wanted to capture the essence of a tiny, claustrophobic space, they could use tight, badly composed angles. Good filmmakers understand and apply rules of composition, but they know when to break the rules.

4:3 Frame

16:9 Frame

4 Units

3 Units

4:3
Standard Video
Resolutions:160 x 120, 320 x 240, 640 x 480...

16 Units

9 Units

16:9
Widescreen Video
Resolutions:640 x 360, 852 x 480, 1280 x 720, 1920 x 1080...

HEY!
Download the
SMA animation
program for FREE

StopmotionExplosion.com

Chapter 7

Animating

You have a story, a set, some lights, a camera and it's time to call ACTION! Learn some basic animation skills with **SMA**, a simple stop motion program.

Stopmotion in 6 Steps

1. The stopmotion software displays an image from the camera Clicking a button in the animation program "grabs" a single frame from the camera.
2. Sets, characters, and props are placed in front of the camera.

Animation Words

Frame rate (fps): The number of frames played per second in the finished animation. Higher frame rates (15-24 fps) will look smoother, but require more time to animate. Animations with lower frame rates (5-12 fps) are faster to create, but look "jerky."

Onion Skinning: Animation programs allow you to look at a number of frames at the same time, by making each frame transparent, and layering it on top of the previous frame.

Compression: Video files take up a lot of space on the computer's disk. Compression makes these files smaller. The software that accomplishes this is called a codec.

Codec: A codec is a piece of software for making a video file smaller. Windows Media Video 9, H.264 and MPEG-4 are popular codecs. Your animation program should allow you to pick from a list of codecs. You probably have several on your computer already, and many more are available as free downloads.

3. The animator moves the characters a tiny amount, pulls their fingers out of the scene and pushes a button in the stopmotion software, "grabbing" a frame from the camera.

4. This process continues until the animator has "grabbed" many frames.

5. The program plays the grabbed frames back, allowing the animator to preview the animation.

6. When the animation is finished the program assembles the frames into a movie file.

Animation Software for Windows and Macs

Several free animation programs are available. In this book, you'll find instructions for two of them: **SMA** and **MonkeyJam**.

If you're a Mac user, your free software options are limited, but do exist! **FrameByFrame** is worth investigating if you're on a tight budget.

While free, FrameByFrame's interface and features are somewhat limited. For those wishing to upgrade, we recommend **iStopMotion**, a shareware program published by Boinx Software.

Introduction to SMA

Assemble your set, gather your actors, place your lights, and plug in your camera. Start SMA by clicking the icon on your desktop, or visiting the directory the program was installed in. After adjusting the camera's focus, image brightness and color, and (assuming the camera is pointed at something you want to animate), click the **Start** button in the upper left corner of the control panel. Congratulations! You've captured the first frame of the animation.

Notice the **Start** button has changed to **Grab**. Click **Grab**, move your actors and props slightly, click **Grab** again, and repeat.

The yellow number in the black window tells you how many frames you've shot. When you've shot a few seconds of video, around 30 or 40 frames, click the *Play* arrow and watch the footage you've created. If you want to add more frames to the animation, continue with more movements and grabs. When your scene is complete, click *Done*, give the file a name, save the file, and you've completed your first animated video!

You don't need to open SMA to play the video after it's been saved to the disk. Just double click the video file. Your computer's media player will launch and start playing what you created.

To catch up on the rest of SMA's abilities, check out the **Advanced Features** section a few pages ahead.

Animation Techniques

The movements of the walk cycle and run cycle are probably the most important actions to master, because most movies feature characters walking or running around.

Blob Animation

Start with a blob of moldable material, like Silly Putty® or clay. You can squish this around, animate it eating LEGO® minifigs, turning into a snake, growing eyes, ears, and a nose, and so on. After messing with blobs for 5 minutes, you'll probably want to move on to a figure with arms and legs.

Walking and Running

Here is a series of pictures showing the exact movements of a walk cycle and a run cycle using a LEGO® figure, commonly called a "minifig." These little plastic people are great to practice with.

Minifig Walk Cycle

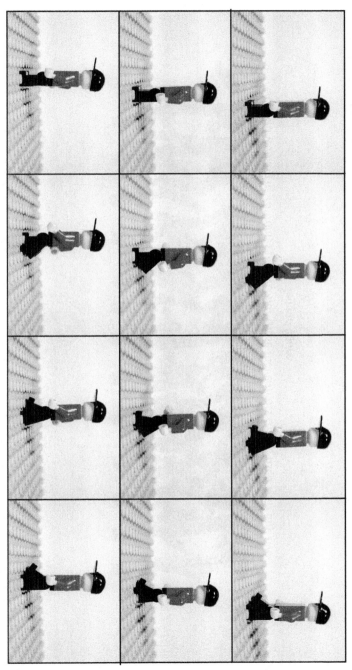

Stikfa Walk Cycle

A stikfa walking at 15 frames per second. These movements can be used with any two-legged figure.

Think. How do you walk? What movements are made? Watch someone walking. How could you break the movements down into minifig size?

Walk Cycle

- The figure's arms swing, but only a little.
- The left arm goes forward with the right foot, and vice versa.
- After the last frame of the sequence above, the figure repeats the cycle, this time leading with the left foot.
- Focus on keeping the minifig's torso upright. Leaning too far forward is a common mistake beginners make.

Minifig Run Cycle

Run Cycle

- The character's arms swing more.
- He leans forward a bit more.

- He covers more ground with each step.
- After the last frame, the cycle begins on the opposite foot.

How Fast? Frames Per Second (FPS)

People walk roughly at two steps every second. Try timing yourself with a stopwatch. To have your stopmotion characters move at the right speed, you'll need to know how many grabs, or "frames," will fill one second of the movie.

Your animation software should have a way to set the "framerate," "fps" or "frames per second." This is the number of frames that fill one second of film. To set the framerate in SMA, click **Options > Capture Options**.

The higher your framerate is, the smoother your animation will appear. However, you'll have to capture all those frames, so animating will take longer.

Most simple animations use a framerate of 10, 12 or 15 FPS.

Animators using 35mm film cameras animate at 12 or 24 fps, as film plays at 24 frames per second. To animate at 12 fps, they simply grab two frames at a time, halving the framerate.

Mouth Animation

Speech can be broken down into individual sounds. These sounds are called Phonemes. This chart shows the shapes the human mouth forms when it sounds out a phoneme.

A character says the phrase:

"Lock the door tonight."

The *Luh, (Lock) Ess, (the) Ooh (door) Ess, Ess (tonight)* shapes would be used to animate this phrase (turn the page to see a picture).

This isn't obvious from the text of the phrase huh? Try saying the phrase yourself in front of a mirror. Look at the shapes your own mouth makes.

Key to making great lip-animation is to focus on how words sound, rather than the letters themselves. Animate sound shapes, not letter shapes.

Mouth shapes do not have to be frame-perfect. The art of lip animation is more impressionistic than exact. The sounds of speech flow together, and the shapes do as well.

Anticipate the sound. Show the mouth shape slightly before the character vocalizes the sound itself. Humans see things before they hear them.

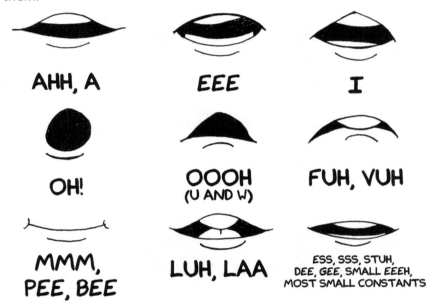

Using a webcam to record and replay your own lip movements while speaking can take the guesswork out of breaking phrases down into individual shapes.

Lips

Adding animated lips to a character can be done in several ways. All lip-animation techniques require the character dialog to be recorded before animating, as the lip shapes and shape-timing is derived from the dialog. The method used depends on the kind of character being animated, and whatever "look" the animator is trying to achieve.

The animator can make several heads, model each head in the phoneme shapes shown here, then swap heads as needed. If a soft material, like clay is being animated, the mouth shapes can be molded into the head. Alternatively, the animator can make just the mouth shapes, and swap out the mouth (this technique is used in the *Wallace and Gromit* films).

Lip shapes added to a character after animating using video compsiting techniques

Mouth shapes can be added after animating, with a video-compositing program, such as **Adobe After Effects.** Using this technique, the characters are animated with blank heads. The mouth-shapes are drawn and composited onto the head after animating.

SMA: Advanced Features

We've given you a very brief summary of SMA. Let's backtrack a bit and take a look at the program's advanced features

After you plug in the camera and start up SMA, the camera window (Live View) may be very small. Resize the window by clicking *Special > Video Window Size...* Make the size of the window *640 x 480*. The

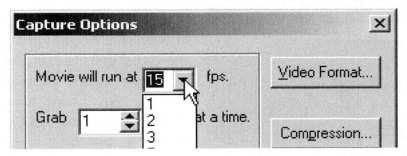

window will become a lot bigger.

Now, let's make sure the frame rate is set at 15 frames per second. Click *Options > Capture Options*, and look at the drop-down menu in the sentence *"Movie will run at xx fps"* where *xx* is a number. Clicking the drop-down menu lets you set higher and lower frame rates.

There are more interesting buttons in the main SMA window, below *Start/Grab* and *Done*.

By dragging the little slider bar back and forth, you can preview individual captured frames. A yellow number will appear, showing the number of the frame you're looking at.

Below the slider bar are different ways to play and rewind your frames. The big button with the circle and arrow lets you loop the frames as they are played.

SMA onion skin interface. The onion button activates the feature, and the slider fades between the live video and last frame captured.

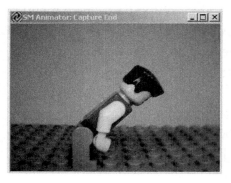

Onion Skinning

When you move a figure, it helps to see how the new position lines up to the last frame captured. Some animation programs give you a way to do this. This feature is called **onion skinning**.

Here's a visual demonstration of onion skinning. The top image shows the last frame captured.

In the second frame the character has bent forward slightly. With onion skinning turned on, the frame and the character's new position have been blended together in the camera window. It's easy to see how far the character has moved.

When the character is in the right place, a frame can be grabbed. You can continue grabbing frames, and previewing the character's position using onion skinning until the animation is complete.

Onion skinning is also handy when you've knocked your character over, and are trying to align the figure with the last frame captured!

The term "onion skinning" is borrowed from traditional cell animation, where drawings were made on thin see-through "onion-skin" paper, allowing the animator to see their previous drawings.

Video Files

The basic Windows file that contains video and sound is called an **AVI** file. SMA creates these files when an animation is saved.

Video players, like **Windows Media Player**, or the open-source **VLC Player**, can open and play AVI files.

The files animation software creates are usually very large compared to ordinary picture and word processing files.

Intelligent Filenames

In the **Story** chapter, we discussed shooting scripts and storyboards. You should remember numbering scenes within the screenplay, and labeling frames in the storyboard with scene and shot numbers.

If you're working from a storyboard, you can name each video clip with the scene and shot number.

If you're animating from a script, name each video clip with the scene number and another number for the shot. Advance the shot number by 1 every time the camera is moved.

Finally, add a "take" number to the end of the filename. Takes are a simple way to track re-animated shots, if you animate a shot once, and decide to animate the same shot again, this is the second "take" of the shot, or "Take 2!"

In the end, you'll get something like this:

MyGreatMovie_Scene4_Shot1_Take1.avi

Looking at this name, we know it's the first take of the first shot in scene 4.

MyGreatMovie_Scene4_Shot1_Take2.avi

The second take of the first shot in scene 4.

MyGreatMovie_Scene8_Shot3_Take1.avi

The first take of the third shot in scene 8, and so on...

If you have plenty of disk space, you may not care about the size of your AVI files. However, the files will need to be "compressed" if you wish to share them with others over the Internet. Compression will make the files smaller. Read on to learn more about this.

Video Formats

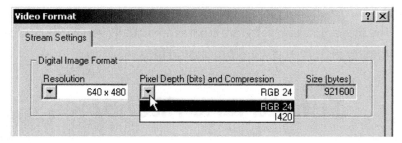

Setting the video format in your animation program affects the size and quality of your video files. To access this menu in SMA, click **Options > Capture Options...** and the **Video Format...** button.

The **"Pixel Depth/Compression"** option lets you choose how the computer saves the numbers that stand for the colors in each pixel. Make sure **RGB24** is selected. If you pick **I420**, or something with **YUV** in it, you can cut the video file size in half, however this can cause problems with the onion skinning feature in SMA. Be aware of this.

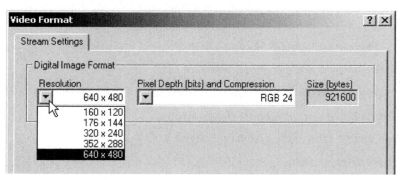

The "Resolution" box lets you choose how many pixels are saved in each individual frame. Remember when we resized the video window to **640 x 480**? We were making the window **640** pixels across and **480** pixels tall. Video sharing websites support resolutions of **640 x 480** and higher, so it's advisable to animate at this resolution. Animate at the largest resolution your computer can handle. You can scale your footage down to smaller resolutions afterwards.

Compression

Compression is a way to make your finished files a lot smaller, even 20 or 40 times smaller!

   Important: If you're using SMA, we don't recommend setting any compression while animating. This can cause problems. Set compression to *Full Frames* by clicking **Options > Capture Options > Compression**. Usually you compress your video clip after animating. We explain how to do this with the VirtualDub program at the end of this book.

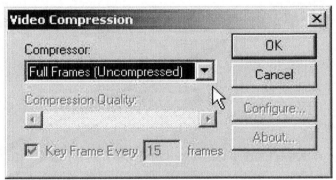

   When choosing a type of compression, you'll get a list of abbreviations. We explain these abbreviations and give some suggestions in the **Files and Formats** chapter.

Miscellaneous Handy Stuff

Several small items that are handy to have within reach while animating.

Tape

Very useful for securing objects that are prone to moving when they shouldn't. Buy the double-sided stuff if you can find it.

Blu-tac/Adhesive Putty

Like clay, except it's not oily and messy. Like tape, it's handy for keeping things in place. You can also stick it on the feet of your characters when they're walking on smooth surfaces or pulling off an acrobatic move, and need extra balance. Art supply stores carry this substance.

Sometimes it's found in stationery aisles.

Tweezers

Handy for moving hard to reach objects in the far corners of your set, without bumping something with your fingers.

Poster board

Sheets in various natural colors make good backgrounds for your scenes. You can cut pieces into clouds, hills, and buildings.

Books, blocks of wood, flat things

These help you raise or lower a set or camera to get the angle you want.

Fun is Important!

Animating requires a lot of patience. Don't animate more than you're capable of in a day. Schedule time to unwind. Otherwise, you'll get sick of animating and loose your creative edge.

Links

SMA:
www.stopmotionexplosion.com
Frame By Frame:
http://web.mac.com/philipp.brendel/Software/FrameByFrame. html
You can download iStopmotion and try the program free for five days:
http://www.boinx.com/istopmotion
MonkeyJam:
http://www.giantscreamingrobotmonkeys.com/monkeyjam/ download.html

Chapter 8

Flight

Special effects in theatrical movies are created by skilled artists. They use sophisticated software, and elaborate equipment. We can achieve similar results with a little elbow grease and creativity.

The digital trickery in this chapter will be done with a paint program or image editor. The program you use must be better than Microsoft Paint. We have a couple of recommendations.

First, **Paint.NET**. The program is free, simple to use, and has many common image-editing tools. We'll be using Paint.Net in this chapter.

GIMP is another free program with powerful features. It also comes in a Mac-compatible flavor.

We decided Paint.NET was the easiest for first-time users to pick up, but if you're already familiar with image editing (or use a Mac) you might prefer GIMP.

You can also use Photoshop, Corel Draw, and many other programs. Your image editor must have these basic features.

1. Layers. You should be able to stack multiple images on top of one another (more on this later).
2. An eraser tool.

Liftoff

The fastest, easiest way to fake small jumps, is to have a character leap partly out of the picture with their first movement, then hold them in place with a pair of tweezers, or your fingers. (You'll probably get your fingers in the picture).

In this chapter, we'll show you how to build and use some rigging to hold your object or character in the air while you animate their aerial antics.

Blank Frame

Before you start animating, capture a single frame of the background you want the character to fly across. This frame will be used later, to accomplish some digital trickery. (This frame can be the first, or last frame of your animation sequence. We'll pull it out of your animation later).

Flying Rigs

After you've captured the "blank frame," go ahead and animate your character flying through the air, held in place with your specially built flying rig. We've given you some designs to start with over the next few pages.

It's very important to make sure the lighting remains consistent throughout the animation, and the background isn't nudged or bumped.

Remember the framerate and resolution of your animation. You'll need this information later.

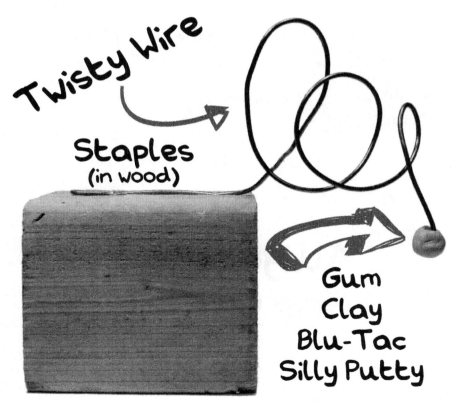

Basic Flying Rigs

Twisty Wire

Staples
(in wood)

Gum
Clay
Blu-Tac
Silly Putty

Funky LEGO
pieces

Stunt Guy

Helping Hands

Alligator
Grip Clips

Flying Rig Techniques

Right Wrong

The object to be animated should be attached to the rig in a place that's not visible from the camera's view.

Pins

Clay

Flying Eraser Head

You can build rigs out of many things. Depending on the size of the object you're supporting, you could even build something out of pins.

Conversion

Finished the animation? The next step will vary, depending on how the animation program you're using saves frames to your computer.

1: Got Image Sequences?

If you're using a program that saves individual image files instead of video files (MonkeyJam does this) you'll need to navigate to the directory the image files are saved in (the default MonkeyJam directory is *Documents > MonkeyJam*). Find this directory, then move on to **3: File Numbers.**

2: Got Video Files?

If you're using a program that saves video files, (SMA does this) you'll need to convert the video file into a series of image files. We explain how to do this with the free VirtualDub program (page over to the VirtualDub chapter at the end of the book and look under the **Converting Video into Pictures** heading). Create the image files and save them somewhere on your computer. **Move to 3: File Numbers**.

3: File Numbers

Number the images in the order they were captured while you were animating. Most animation programs and VirtualDub will do this automatically. The first image should be your blank image, the one you captured before you started animating.

Got your image files? Great. Let's start editing them!

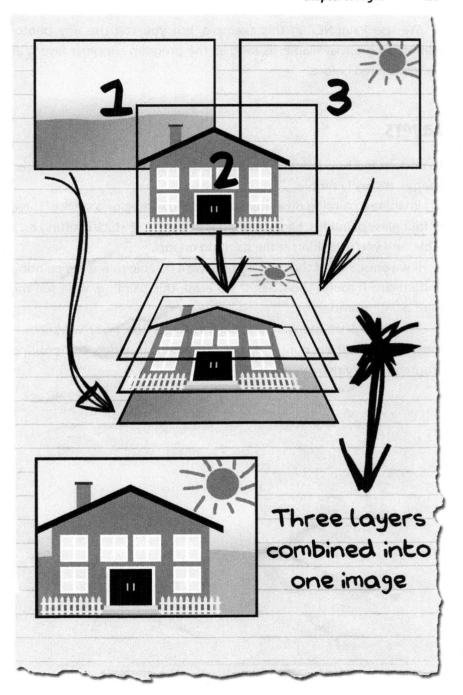

Three layers combined into one image

We use Paint.NET in this example, but you can use any photo-editing program available, as long as the program supports layers, as we mentioned before.

Layers

To understand how Paint.NET works, you'll need to understand layered images. It's really simple.

Imagine a painting on a sheet of glass. Now imagine a stack of three or four glass paintings. Each painting is a "layer." The stack is sitting on a table, and you're looking at the painting on top.

If we erase half of the top painting, we'll be able to see the painting underneath through the glass. If we erase this painting, we'll see the third painting, and so on.

Take a look at the diagram on this page. The layer workflow is something you'll encounter again and again, in video compositing programs, and video editors.

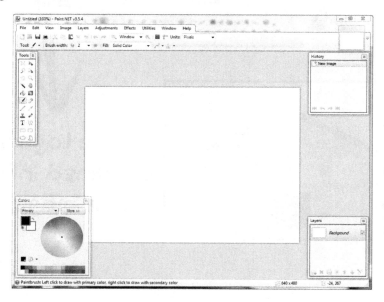

Begin the Edit

Start up Paint.NET, or the image editor of your choice.

First, we'll create a new image. Click **File > New**. Set the resolution of the image to the resolution of the image files you will be editing. Our images have a width of **640**, and a height of **480**. Leave everything else at the default settings.

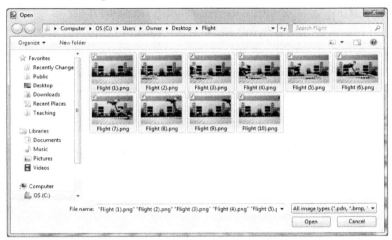

Click **Layers > Import from File**. Navigate to the location where you saved all those animation image files earlier. Select all the images by hitting **Ctrl +A**.

Before you click **Open**, notice how we've numbered our files in the order they were animated. This ensures they will be imported into Paint.NET in the correct order.

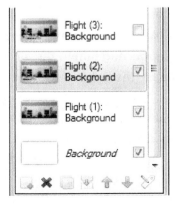

The images will load into Paint.NET as layers. You'll see them appearing in the Layer window. If you don't see this window, click **Window > Layers**, or hit **F7**.

Familiarize yourself with this window, because you'll be using it a lot. Uncheck, or "hide" all the layers except the first two layers, and the bottom *background* layer. You can see how we've done this in the picture below (on the left).

As mentioned earlier, we've numbered the layers in the order they appeared in the original animation. The "Flight (1)" layer is the frame with nothing in it, the frame you captured before starting to animate with your flying rig. "Flight (2)" is the first frame with the flying rig. The *background* frame is a blank, white frame with nothing in it. You can ignore this layer.

On the left side of the paint program, you should see a window with paint tools. If not click **Window > Tools**, or hit **F5**. Click the **Eraser** tool.

Tool: ✐ ▾ | Brush width: ⊖ 40 ▾ ⊕

You'll need to adjust the width of the eraser, so you're not erasing tiny dots. Adjust the brush width until it's medium sized.

Return to the Layers window. Click the second layer, so it's highlighted as in the picture. This is important.

In the image window, you should see your "flying" character, and some of the rig supporting him in the air. Let's erase the rig!

Click, and start erasing. Erase until the rig is completely gone. Pretty amazing huh?

Save this image by clicking **File > Save As...**

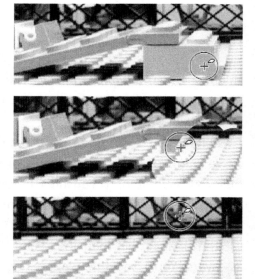

Erasing the rig. Adjust the width of the brush to erase the tricky spots, where the rig touches the character.

Here's where things get a little wonky. In the *Save as type* drop-down menu, click PNG. This is the first frame of our flight animation, so name it "AnimationFlight_1.png" or something similar. Numbering your saved frames is very important, as this will allow you to re-assemble them into a video file later! Click *Save*. You might get a *Save Configuration* window. Go with the default settings and click OK.

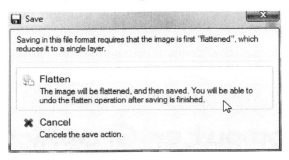

You'll see this window appear. Click *Flatten*. The image will save... but HEY! Where did all our layers go?

Don't worry. They're still hanging around. Click *Edit > Undo*, and the layers will pop back like they never left.

If you're using a program like Photoshop, you'll be able to "save a copy," which saves a PNG file and preserves the original layers. Unfortunately, Paint. NET doesn't have this feature, so we'll be using the aforementioned workaround.

Next step. In the Layer window, uncheck the layer you just edited, and check the layer immediately above it. Make sure the layer is selected by clicking it, as pictured.

Go ahead and erase the rig in this image. Make sure you're cleaning up any shadows, and pay special attention to areas where the rig goes behind your character, or intersects with it.

Save, following the steps of the workaround mentioned previously, and continue on to the next layer.

If you're having problems erasing parts of the layer, (you erase, and erase, but nothing happens) chances are, you haven't selected the layer first, by clicking it in the Layers panel. <u>You can only edit a layer if it's selected!</u>

Erase the rig in all the frames of your animation. You can zoom in and out with the magnifying glass tool, and adjust the width of the eraser for finer control. If you mess up and erase the wrong thing, hit *Ctrl+Z*.

Computer Graphics

Bit: One digit of a number stored in a computer. It can be either 1 or 0. Most computers now store a color as a 24 bit number—8 bits for the amount of red, 8 for green and 8 for blue. This is called "RGB24" color.

Bitmap: Contains the bits that stand for the colors of every pixel in a picture, arranged in order starting at one corner. The files contain a lot of information and are very large.

JPEG & PNG: Contain bits that represent the colors in a picture. Instead of one bit for every pixel, the bits may stand for areas of color or for changes between a pixel and the pixels surrounding it. This makes the filesize much smaller.

Conversion Take Two

After you finish erasing the rig in every image, you'll have a folder of edited images. If you've followed the instructions so far, you've numbered them in the order they appear. The last step is converting the images into a video file. This can be done easily with **Virtual Dub**.

For a detailed explanation of Virtual Dub, turn to the chapter at the end of the book. Here's a super-condensed version of the steps you'll take:

Fire up VirtualDub. Click *File* > *Open video file...* make sure the "Automatically load linked segments" box in the lower left corner is checked. Select the first image, and click *Open*. The entire sequence of images will load into VirtualDub.

Before saving the pictures as a video file, make sure the frame rate is set correctly, by clicking *Video* > *Frame rate...* Change it to the correct speed. (If you animated at 15 frames per second, the frame rate will be 15). Click *OK*.

Set the compression, (click *Video* > *Compression*), and create the video (click *File* > *Save as...* type in a name and click *Save*).

Pat yourself on the back. You're amazing.

This compositing technique has many uses. Instead of using the eraser, as we did in this example, you could use a paint tool, and draw explosions, or graphic effects on frames. You can remove the background from pictures of objects and place the object into your animation. With a little practice, it's possible to composite moving mouths and expressions on characters.

If you find yourself compositing a lot of frames, you should move to a dedicated video compositing program, like **After Effects**, or **DebugMode's Wax 2.0** (a free program).

Chroma Key Effects

Chroma-keying is another way to create the appearance of flight.

You may have seen blue and green screens placed behind actors and objects in movie studios. The chroma-key effect is used to place a TV weatherman in front of a huge radar display, and insert model planes in clouds high above the earth.

Some video editors come with a chroma-key effect that can be applied to footage with a green or blue background. Unfortunately, Windows Movie Maker, the free editing program for Windows does not

Before

After

have a way to chroma-key footage at this time.

Shoot footage with a solid green background behind your figure. You can choose blue or red as well. Pick a color that is different from all the colors in the object you wish to chroma key.

Choose a scene you want behind the character. This can be a still picture, graphic, or a live video clip.

Place your greenscreen clip and the clip you wish to appear behind your character on the video editor's timeline. Video editors with chroma-key abilities often have two or more video tracks. You'll place the greenscreen clip on the top track, and the second clip on the bottom track.

Select the chroma-key effect and apply it to the greenscreen clip. The effect analyzes the footage and makes solid colors transparent. In this example, all green color in the clip will become transparent, revealing the new background behind your character.

Study your video editor's manual to learn more of the chroma key's controls and parameters. These will improve the quality of your "key."

The free Wax 2.0 compositing program is often recommended for basic chroma key operations. You can find many tutorials for using the program on YouTube, and the Internet.

Links

Paint.NET
www.getpaint.net
GIMP
www.gimp.org
Wax 2.0
www.debugmode.com/wax/

Chapter 9

Animating With MonkeyJam

MonkeyJam is a great piece of animation freeware written by David Perry. It's designed for previewing "pencil tests," scanned pencil drawings that cel animators create before inking and painting the frames of an animation.

Of special interest to stopmotion junkies, MonkeyJam has a video interface that allows you to grab images directly from a camera!

We have discussed the SMA animation program, but you may decide to use MonkeyJam instead. It's completely up to you. We recommend using the program with the features and interface that appeal to you the most.

After you download and install MonkeyJam, plug your camera into the computer and click that adorable monkey icon. You'll see a window like this:

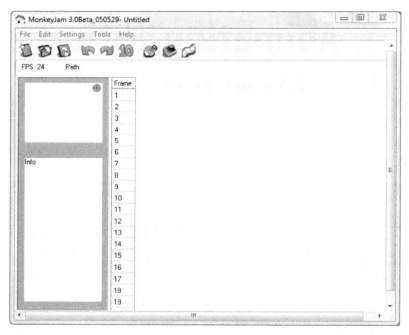

If you've used SMA before, the MonkeyJam interface will look very different. Where's the video preview window, grab button and playback controls?

These controls are here, hidden in the program's menus. Before we start using the animation controls, we'll introduce one of MonkeyJam's most powerful features, the **Exposure Sheet**.

Exposure Sheet is sometimes shortened to **x-sheet** or **XPS**. The x-sheet keeps track of the frames in your animation, the order in which they appear, the framerate, and other bits of information.

Click *File > New XPS with folders...*

A window will pop up. For the *Project Name*, type in something like "MyGreatAnimation."

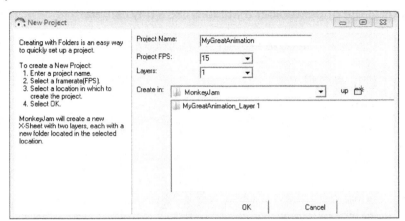

Set the framerate for this animation. In the *Project FPS* drop-down menu, select a number. We recommend 15 FPS. You can choose a custom framerate by clicking *Other*. You can change the x-sheet framerate later by clicking *Settings > FPS*.

Leave *Layers* set to *1*. If we were animating a series of pencil drawings, we might use two layers, but for a stopmotion project, we only need one.

All the images you capture from the camera need to be stored on the computer somewhere. We created a folder called "MonkeyJam" in our Documents folder for the MonkeyJam project files and images.

Finally, click *OK*. You've created your first x-sheet!

*For a complete description of framerates and other animating terminology, flip back to the **Animating** chapter.*

Animation

Let's start animating. Click **Tools** > **Capture** > **Video**, or click that thingy in the upper toolbar that looks like a tiny camera

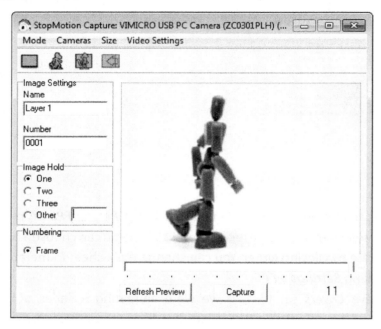

The **Capture** window will pop up. First thing we gotta do is select our camera. Click **Cameras** at the top of the window, and select your model from the drop-down menu.

An image from the camera will appear in the video preview window.

Our stopmotion experience will be more fun if we switch the video window over to **Stop Motion** mode. Click **Mode** > **Stop Motion**.

Excellent! The video window should now look like the image here.

Before clicking that tempting **Capture** button, pay attention to the fields of information on the left side of this window.

- **Name:** This is the name of the image file that will be saved on your computer. You should change it to something relevant, like *"SuperGreatMovieClip01."*

- **Number**: Every image file you save will have an image number, derived from the order the image was captured in. If you needed to change the numbering scheme to prevent overwriting existing images – for example, starting at 0501 instead of 0001, simply type in the number you wish the first frame to have. More about this later. For now, just leave it set at 0001.

- **Image Hold**: This should be set to *One*. MonkeyJam allows you to change the amount of time an image remains on the screen. For example, if you wanted one image to be visible for 5 frames, you could enter *5* in the *Other* text field. You can change the length of individual frames later, in the x-sheet. We'll show you how to do this.

You can change the image resolution by clicking *Size*, and selecting a number between *160 x 120* and *640 x 480*.

You can also access the camera controls menu by clicking *Video Settings > Camera Dialogs* (look carefully for this one! It's in the top toolbar)

It's time to animate!

Frames can be grabbed from the camera by clicking the *Capture* button. Go ahead. Animate a few frames of something. Move your character slightly, pull your fingers out of the picture, click *Capture*, move your character again, click *Capture*, and so on.

Backup!

To back up a MonkeyJam project, you'll need to make copies of the .XPS file and image folder.

For example, this project "MyGreatAnimation" has the MyGreatAnimation. xps file, and a folder of images named MyGreatAnimation_Layer 1. Both of these need to be backed up.

Deleting Frames

After you've captured about ten frames, try clicking and dragging the little slider bar backwards. The last few frames you grabbed will cycle through the video preview window. Additionally, you'll notice the capture button changes.

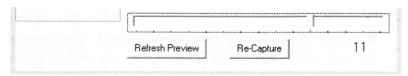

Re-Capture. If you click this button, you'll be able to replace the current frame with a new one from the camera. This is handy if you've accidentally captured a frame with your finger in it. You can also remove frames in the MonkeyJam x-sheet.

Let's return to the main MonkeyJam window.

Playback

The orange column displays a list of frames captured from the camera. You can click on individual frames to preview them.

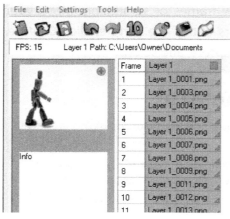

You probably want to preview the entire animation. To do so, click the little TV screen icon at the top, or click *Tools > Preview.* Even faster, hit *F7.*

The Preview window will launch. Click the little right-facing arrow to render and play a preview of your animation.

The animation will loop until you hit the square *Stop*

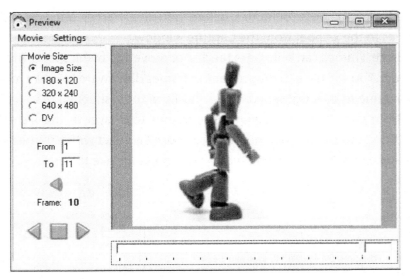

button. You can play the animation backwards by hitting the left-facing arrow. There are more interesting options to experiment with in the *Settings* menu at the top of this window.

Let's take another look at the x-sheet in the main MonkeyJam window.

Moving Frames

Look at the orange column of frames. Try clicking and dragging the tiny corner of the bottommost frame. Drag it downward until it spans about five or so frames.

Now click the little TV button, or hit *F7* to render another preview. The last frame should holds for five frames.

You can do this with any frame in the x-sheet. Multiple frames can be selected and moved around by clicking, holding down the *Shift* key, and clicking again. You can change the order of frames, delete individual frames, and add more frames to the x-sheet from the Capture window.

Note: Frames can only be extended or moved to blank spaces in the x-sheet. You will have to drag a stack of frames downward to make room for a frame to be lengthened in the middle of the x-sheet.

Note also: If you're adding more frames to a layer in the x-sheet, you'll need to ensure their numbering doesn't conflict with a frame that already exists. If this happens, you'll see a message like this:

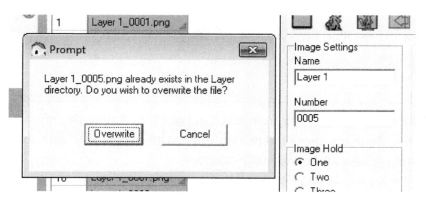

You can ensure this doesn't happen by changing the **Number** or the **Name** in the capture window.

Additionally, MonkeyJam will try adding frames wherever there's a blank space in the x-sheet. For example, if there's a gap between frame 2 and frame 6. MonkeyJam will try inserting frames into this gap. If you want frames to be added to the end of your animation, make sure these gaps are closed up.

Audio and MonkeyJam

You can import .**WAV** audio files into MonkeyJam. This is extremely useful when you're trying to animate characters with moving lips, matching the animation to the dialog.

You can import a sound file by clicking *File* > *Import* > *Audio* (MonkeyJam does not support *MP3s*.)

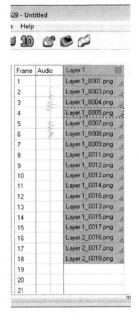

You'll see a track of audio appear, running parallel to the frames in your x-sheet. If you were to preview your movie, the audio would play along with the frames. You can also play or "scrub" the audio. Click a frame in the audio track, hold the mouse button down, and drag the mouse downward.

If you look close at the audio track, you'll see squiggle lines. These squiggles are called waveforms. Waveforms are a visualization of audio. They are discussed further in the **Sound** chapter. For now, know that sound happens wherever these lines appear in the audio track.

If you double-click a frame in the audio track, you'll notice a text

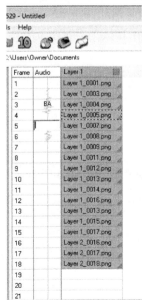

field appears. You can add little reminders and notes here by typing and hitting *Enter*. This is especially useful when you're matching character animation to a dialog recording, or you're animating a character with moving lips – you can add notes reminding yourself where phoneme shapes occur in a section of dialog.

MonkeyJam has an upper limit of 1637 frames in an x-sheet. Sooner or later, you'll need to export an AVI file for further editing. In the main window, click the little icon that looks like a strip of film, or hit *File* > *Export Avi...*

A save file dialog will pop up.

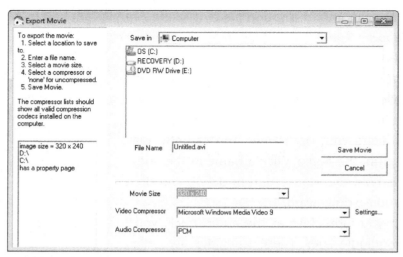

The *Movie Size* should match the *Image Size* property on the left. Choose a suitable video codec – you can see we're using Microsoft Windows Media Video 9. Finally, pick an audio compressor. If your x-sheet does not contain any sound, click *None*.

Finally, MonkeyJam comes with an excellent help file. You can access this information by hitting *F1* or clicking *Help* in the main window.

This concludes the MonkeyJam demonstration. It's a great program with many solid features.

Links

Monkeyjam:

www.giantscreamingrobotmonkeys.com/monkeyjam/index.html

Chapter 10

The Art of War

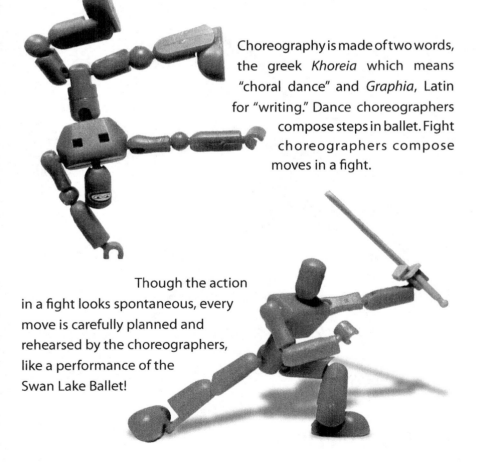

Choreography is made of two words, the greek *Khoreia* which means "choral dance" and *Graphia*, Latin for "writing." Dance choreographers compose steps in ballet. Fight choreographers compose moves in a fight.

Though the action in a fight looks spontaneous, every move is carefully planned and rehearsed by the choreographers, like a performance of the Swan Lake Ballet!

Fight Arc Graph

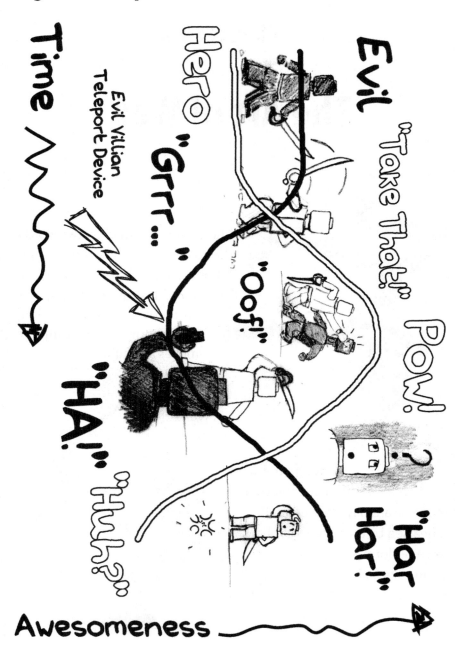

Think about dancing. If two people are dancing together, one makes a movement and their partner responds. Fighting is very similar. One person throws a punch, and their opponent reacts by blocking, dodging, or returning the blow.

As a choreographer, you'll decide what weapons and fighting styles are used, how long the fight lasts, and how the fight will arc from beginning to end.

Arcs are simple to understand. Take a look at one here. The best stories use fights to help the audience understand the hero and villain.

The hero loses his first battles because he's flawed. Maybe he's over confident, or doesn't understand the problem he's facing. The villain is really evil and tough to beat. After being defeated several times, the hero "gets it," addresses his fatal flaws, and comes back to win.

As an exercise, take another look at the fight arc. Do you think this fight teaches the audience something about the hero and villain? Why, or why not?

Check It Out!

Here is a graph of a duel between an evil genius scientist, and a white-suited hero, of average intellegence. On the graph, time is plotted horizontally, awesomeness vertically.

As the hero gets the upper hand, his level of awesomeness goes up. The villian's arc of awesomeness starts going down.

Just when it looks like the villian will be defeated, he reveals his secret teleporter. The villian's arc goes up, and the hero's arc goes down, just as the episode ends. Tune in next time...

You've Got Moves

Punches and kicks should be snappy. There's a little anticipation, as the figure prepares to throw the punch, which moves very quickly, and a pause, as the figure recovers from the punch.

While animating, make your fight clips short. Break each movement into a single segment that can be re-animated several times if needed. It may take some experimentation to perfect the right balance of anticipation, swing, reaction, and recovery.

In a fight with multiple attackers, the central figure bounces between the attackers until they are defeated, much like a pinball bouncing around a pinball machine.

Let's look at a few frame-by-frame breakdowns of animated punches.

LEGO® & Stikfa Action

LEGO® minifigs are movement-challenged. Their arms and legs can't do what people do.

Exaggerating punches makes them more convincing. The minifig throws their whole body into the blow. The same applies to a minifig taking a punch. They react with their whole body.

Check out some breakdowns over the next few pages.

Right Body Strike

Suit Guy is knocked back, arms trailing as he flies. Landing, he slides slightly.

Uppercut

White Ninja bops Suit Guy on the chin.

Left Hook

Suit Guy comes around with the punch. Notice slight White Ninja reaction before impact.

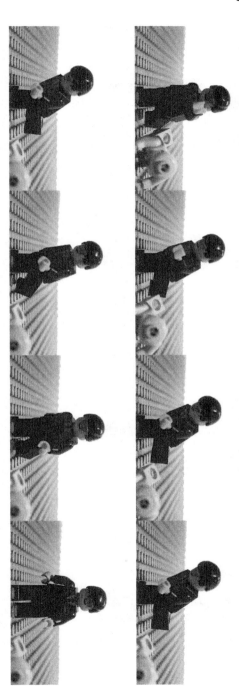

Right Body Strike

Simple, straight punch. The punched character's head should snap back, as shown here.

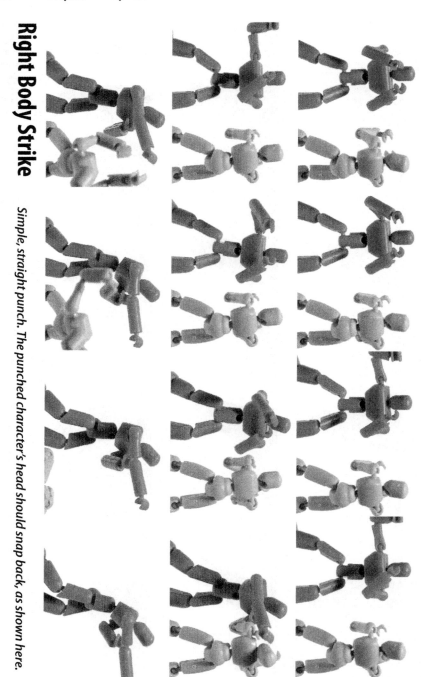

Roundhouse Kick

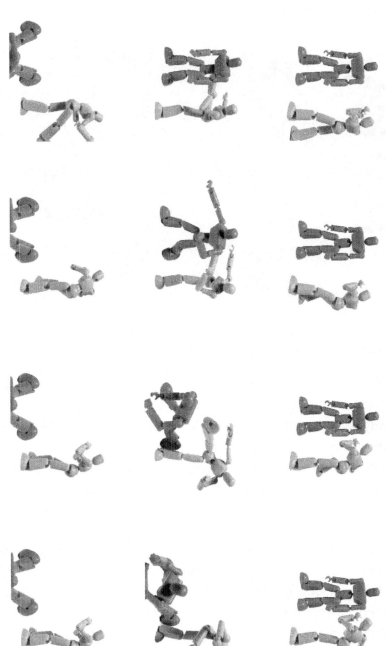

Roundhouse kick to the back. Double-sided tape is extremely useful for these poses..

Keeping it Real Fake

Most of the punches and kicks thrown by stuntman don't connect. Instead, their opponent reacts as if they've been punched, snapping their body backwards. This saves the producers lots of hospital bills, and keeps the performers alive for another show.

You're working with toys and figures that don't care if they've been punched. Should they pummel each other with everything they've got?

Maintaining the speed of a punch will require spacing between frames that doesn't allow a fist or foot (or tentacle/claw/beak) to connect in a frame. This is especially true if you're animating at a lower framerate, say 10-15 FPS. You'll be animating a frame immediately *after* a punch connects. If you look at frame 8 of the Uppercut breakdown, you'll see an excellent example of a non-connecting punch. What's the solution to this dilemma? Sound effects!

Sound Effects

Think about the Amazing Spiderman™. Comic books have BAM! and POW! inked in big, bold letters because...

A punch needs to SOUND like a punch!

This applies to animated and live action films. That crisp "POW" from the Lone Ranger's fist is a recording of someone punching a raw steak with a leather glove (for extra slap). No kiddin'. Sound effects add extra weight to fighting action. Be sure to sprinkle a generous helping into the mix while editing your film. Learn about sound in the next chapter.

Explosions

A thug pulls out his pocket RPG. The hero swings his katana just in time to deflect the missile, which skips across the ground and collides with a propane truck sitting under a critical fuel supply line. How will you animate all that boom?

In today's live-action films, explosions are filmed on site, composited in after filming, or created with a combination of both methods. For many years, stopmotion was used primarily for creating effects in live action films, including explosions. Here are some helpful tips for animating explosions in your own productions using odds and ends from around the house.

Black & White

Capture one bright over-exposed frame, then one under-exposed frame immediately before animating the body of an explosion. Point a light directly into the camera for the light frame, or crank the exposure up. Turn all the set lights off for the dark frame or cover the camera lens. This is a traditional cartooning technique, and adds extra punch to an explosion.

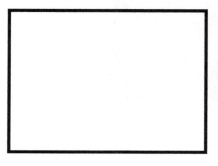

Cotton Wool

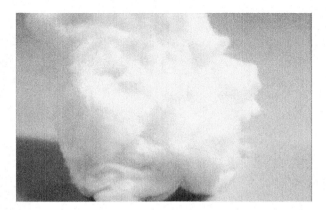

You can buy bags of little cotton balls at cosmetic shops, or "quilt batting" from craft stores. This fluffy stuff forms the explosion cloud. Pull the cotton apart, slowly adding more in each frame until the explosion is big enough, then continue pulling the cotton apart and removing pieces until it drifts out of the frame. Check out the frame-by-frame example on the next page.

Flashlight

Flashlights are useful for creating the glowing heart of an explosion. You can use them with cotton (point the light in the middle of the cloud) or create small spot explosions without the cloud.

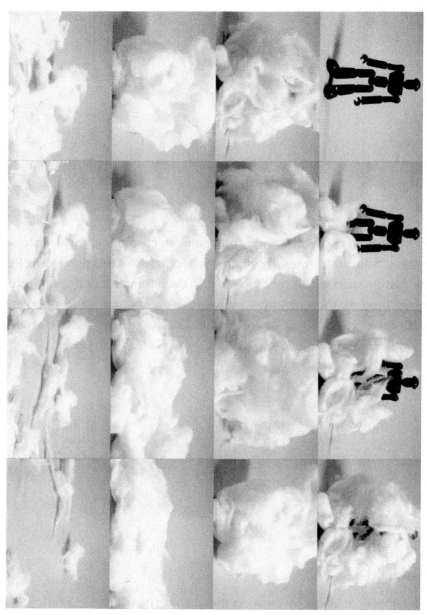

Cotton Wool Smoke Breakdown

Example: The Rocket

Five...four...three...two...one... wait! Your moon explorers are grounded if their rocket doesn't have some propellant! This simple effect will get them to the stars and back again.

Build a rocket with a hollow body. Cardboard tubes work well. Use tape or wire to attach your rocket to a flashlight, with the flashlight pointing down, through the rocket body (see illustration).

Turn the flashlight on. Hold your "rocket" by the flashlight handle. Start capturing frames and raising the rocket into the air. Use cotton smoke below the rocket to enhance the effect.

Paper

Paper cutouts can be used to create small explosions. Grab a sheet of cardstock, construction paper, or posterboard, if your cutout will be very large.

Create several cutouts of progressing size, one for each stage of the explosion, and insert the cutouts into the scene, one frame at a time, starting with the smallest and ending with the largest.

Here's an animation of a water main breaking, made with six construction-paper cutouts (check out the breakdown on the next page). Note how the animation alternates between two cutouts in the last six frames, creating the illusion of leaping water.

Papermation Water Spray Breakdown

Gunfire

Firing a gun creates muzzle flash, a small explosion from the tip of the gun. The gun kicks back, moving the gunman's arm slightly each time it's fired.

You can animate a muzzle flash and the arm movement using a combination of the techniques we've introduced so far. These effects should be visible for about one frame, if you're animating at 15 FPS. Add a gunshot sound effect during the edit.

Flashlight Blast

Really basic. A flashlight pointed into the set for one or two frames. Combining this technique with the other effects here will produce a better effect.

Paper Blast

A paper cutout of a muzzle flash. Post-it notes are great for this. Cut the flash out of the post-it so that the sticky part is the end that attaches to the muzzle of the gun.

Cotton Blast

The blast of a black powder flintlock pistol, with cotton wool smoke. Use a little glue from a glue stick to attach the wool to the muzzle. The "smoke" should be visible for several frames, appearing quickly, as the gun is fired, and slowly drifting away afterwards.

Enhanced Blast

We've made the flashlight blast a little more impressive by drawing a muzzle flash into the frame with Paint.NET. Keep reading for more details.

LEGO® Blaster

When you visit galaxies far, far away, everyone is packing their favorite blaster-gas projectile accessory. If you're animating with a construction toy, you can use a long thin piece for the blaster beam, like this transparent LEGO® antenna. Since the piece is visible for a single frame, it will look like a "real" laser beam.

Knitting Needle Blaster

You can use any long, thin object as a blaster beam, like knitting needles. Use your fingers, or another character to support the other end of the needle offscreen.

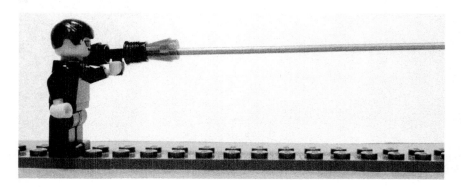

Paint.NET Blaster

We introduced Paint.NET in the previous chapter, showing how to create the illusion of flight by erasing supports using the program's layers and image-editing tools.

You can also use Paint.NET to draw obects into frames. Here's a way to draw and animate blaster fire, the kind you see in a Star Wars film.

Read the introduction to Paint.NET, if you haven't done so already. Following the tutorial, convert your animation into frames (if needed), start Paint.NET, create a new image with the same resolution as your animation, import your images as layers and hide all the layers except the one containing the first frame of your animation.

Now, at the bottom of the Layers window, click the "Add New Layer" button, which looks like a little square with a plus mark on the corner.

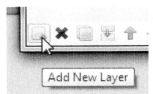

This will add a new blank layer to the stack of layers in the Layer window. We need to move this layer to the top of the stack. Select the new layer by clicking it, and click the little arrow pointing up, until the new layer is on top.

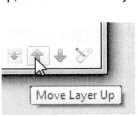

Finally, double-click this new layer (pictured here, as **Layer 7**) and rename it "Blaster Layer" in the Layer Properties window.

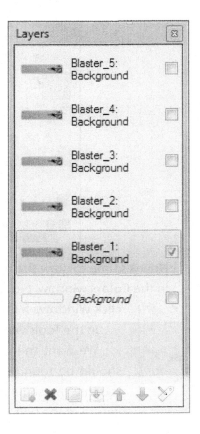

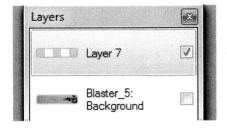

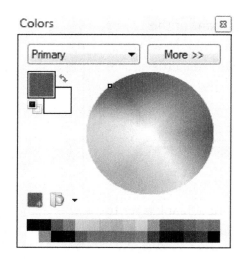

Now it's time to draw the blaster bolt.

In the **Colors** window, pick a nice blue. If you don't see this window, click **Windows > Colors**.

In the Tools window, click the **Lines / Curves** tool.

We want the line to look like a blaster bolt. The ends should be rounded, and the width of the bolt should be roughly the same as the width of the blaster muzzle. The length of the bolt is entirely up to you.

In this example, we've made the width of the brush 35 pixels, and set both ends of the line to be rounded using the two drop-down menus in the Style area.

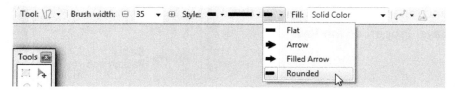

To draw the bolt, click and drag the mouse in a straight line away from the blaster muzzle.

Holding the **Shift** key down while you drag the mouse will draw a perfectly straight line.

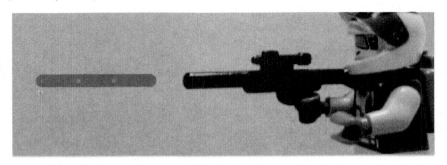

A blaster bolt has a white-hot center surrounded by a colored corona (an effect caused by superheated particles releasing energy into the environment as light... did we mention there'll be a test at the end of the week?) We'll blur the edges of the line we just drew, creating the corona, and recolor the center for that white-hot effect. Click **Effects > Blur > Gaussian Blur...**

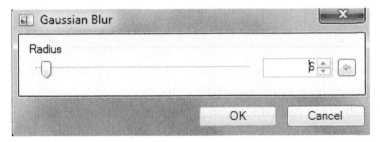

Use enough blur to make the edges of the bolt fuzzy. We've set a radius of 6 pixels, but you can experiment. Click OK.

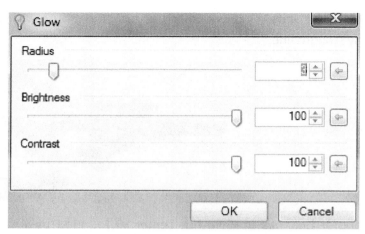

Now, click **Effects > Photo > Glow**.

Crank the Brightness and Contrast up to 100, giving the bolt a white center. Set the radius to around 3 pixels, so a nice rim of blue is visible around the edge of the bolt.

You can increase the amount of glow by clicking **Effects > Repeat Glow...** but this may decolor the corona.

Finally, (you can skip this step, but it makes the bolt look nicer) add some motion blur. Click **Effects > Blurs > Motion Blur...**

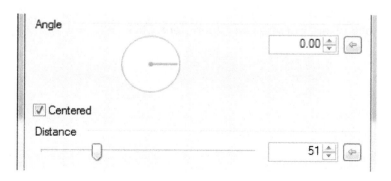

Set the angle of the blur to be the direction the bolt is traveling. Our bolt is traveling straight across the screen, so the angle is 0. If the bolt was traveling straight towards the top of the screen, we would set the angle to 90. To set the angle correctly, simply drag the line inside the Angle circle around so the line is pointing in the direction the bolt is moving.

The distance of the blur in pixels should be great enough to leave a nice "tail" around the bolt. Try a value of 40-50. It might take a few seconds to render the blur.

Why not add a little muzzle flash too? To create the effect below, make a new layer, paint over the muzzle using a large white brush, and applied the Gaussian Blur filter to the layer (**Effects > Blur > Gaussian Blur...**), with a radius of 45 pixels. The flash is visible for one frame.

One frame of our blaster bolt animation is complete. Save the frame by clicking **File > Save As...**

If you followed the Paint.NET tutorial prior to reading this chapter, you'll remember there's a trick to saving images in Paint.NET. In the "Save as type" drop-down menu, click PNG. This is the first frame of our blaster animation. Name it "Blaster_Fire01.png." Don't forget to number the frames as you save them!

Click *Save*. You might get a "Save Configuration" window. Go with the default settings and click OK.

This window will appear. Click "Flatten." The image will save, and your layers will disappear. Click **Edit > Undo**, and they'll pop back again.

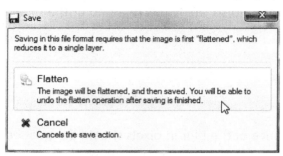

Paint.NET, and most image and video programs that use layers allow the position of a layer to be adjusted independently of all the other layers. This is very useful. Instead of drawing a new blaster bolt ahead of the bolt we just created and erasing the old one, we can move the old blaster bolt forward, and save the results!

Creating the next frame of the animation is very simple. Hide the current frame, the one we just exported, by un-checking the checkbox next to it in the Layer window. Reveal the next frame by checking its box. Leave the box next to the Blaster Layer checked (see illustration opposite).

In the Tools window, click the **Move Selected Pixels** button. Make sure the blaster layer is selected by clicking it. Click the blaster bolt somewhere in the middle. Drag the bolt forward, releasing it when it's roughly twice the distance away from the muzzle it was in the previous frame.

Save this frame, following our previously outlined steps. Move the blaster bolt forward in each frame in your animation. When

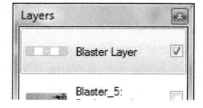

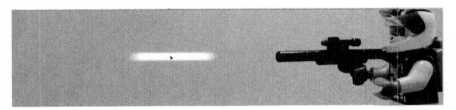

you are finished, assemble the individual frames into a movie file using VirtualDub.

If you are animating more than one blaster bolt in a frame of your animation, draw each bolt on a separate layer. You can customize blaster bolts by drawing the initial line in different colors. We used blue. Try yellow, red and green.

This technique can also be used to create lightsaber effects. First, animate your figures battling with solid, straight rods. Draw the lightsaber "blade" over the rods. Draw each blade on a different layer. The layer with the blade closest to the camera should be on top. When the blades clash, insert a white frame, then a black frame, and finally, paint in a large flash with the gaussian blur method used to give the blaster a muzzle flash. This flash should last a couple of frames.

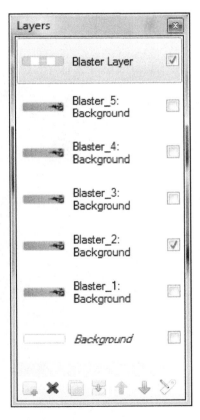

Chapter 11

Sound

Straight from the camera, stopmotion films have no audio. You may love the silent film classics of the 1920s, but you want characters with voices in your movies!

Microphones

Many computers have built-in microphones. This microphone can be a great solution for your first film; however it's preferable to use a microphone that plugs into your computer. Doing so will allow you to bring the microphone closer to sound sources and voices.

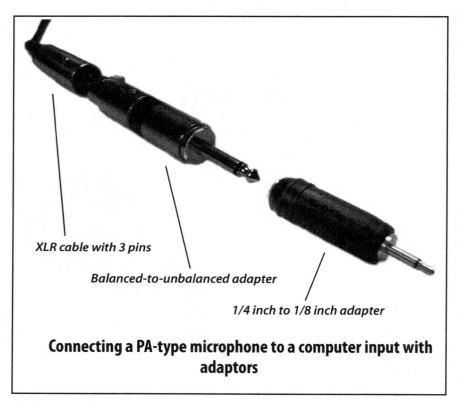

XLR cable with 3 pins

Balanced-to-unbalanced adapter

1/4 inch to 1/8 inch adapter

Connecting a PA-type microphone to a computer input with adaptors

If you don't have a microphone, visit the nearest computer store, or hit eBay. Microphones for Windows and Mac systems are inexpensive and easy to find.

If you have access to a regular PA style microphone, you can acquire an adapter that converts the three-prong microphone connector into the computer's miniature audio connector. The adapter pictured was bought at Radio Shack.

Additionally, USB XLR interfaces can be purchased. This is basically a box that sits between the microphone and computer. The microphone's

XLR cable plugs into the box, and the box interfaces with the computer via USB.

Once your microphone is plugged in, you can launch your audio recording program. For starters, try using the **Windows Sound Recorder**, which comes with all Windows installations, typically found in the **Start** menu, under **Accessories**.

If you've ever used a tape recorder, Sound Recorder doesn't need much explanation. Click the round record button to start recording sound. If you're using Windows Vista, or Windows 7, this window will look a lot simpler

If your sound is very quiet, or sounds bad, try increasing the volume, or changing settings in the **Hardware and Sound** section of the Windows control panel.

OS X users can use the **GarageBand** application to record sounds from their microphone, or the free **Audacity** program. We've included instructions for using Audacity at the end of this chapter.

Recording Sessions

When professional sound mixers do a "tech scout," they listen for nearby traffic, look for refrigerators to unplug, and worry about water running through pipes.

A real recording studio has carefully placed blocks of foam that deaden echos, and special soundproof recording booths. Your recording equipment isn't very sensitive, especially if you're recording sound with the computer's built-in microphone, but try to isolate yourself from unwanted noise. Find a quiet environment to work in.

Recording Sound Effects

If you purchase an MP3 recorder, or MP3 player with an internal microphone, you can record sounds anywhere. Audacity's effects, which you'll learn how to use later in the chapter, can transform boring sounds into very exotic imitations. Here are a few ideas to get you started:

- **Punch** - Pile of jackets and gloves hit with baseball bat. You can hit many objects with sticks, bats, and record great sounds.
- **Snakes Slithering** - Fingers run through cheese casserole.
- **Rock Rolling** - Car coasting, pitch lowered.
- **Rats** - Chickens, high pitched.
- **Earth Cracking** - Balloons rubbed together, pitch lowered.
- **Fire** - Crackling cellophane. Pitch down slightly, and mix with sticks snapping.
- **Ghosts** - Dolphins, pitch raised
- **Large Explosion** - Wind rumble (blowing into mic), pitch lowered.
- **Elevator Door** - File cabinet drawer (add bell ding).
- **Bird Wings** - Leather gloves, flap them in air.
- **Snow** - Carpet laid over gravel, corn starch in container.
- **Monster** - Slide straw in and out of McDonald's cup. Pitch lowered.
- **Sword Swoosh** - Spin a rope through the air, past the microphone. Sticks can also be used.

- **Large Crash** - Set tin cans and other noisemaking items on stepladder stairs, tip them over.
- **Baseball hit** - Match snapping.

It might be tough to record dolphins yourself. Not to worry. Check out the sound effect collections at the end of this chaper.

Recording Dialog

Grab your script and some voice talent. Family and friends are great sources of talent, especially if they enjoy reading books aloud with all the character's voices, or walk around the house repeating quotes from favorite films in odd, high-pitched voices.

It's not ideal to have a crowd of people huddled around one microphone saying their lines. It's better to record one character's lines individually, then move to the next character. This will reduce noise, and allow each performer to get close to the microphone.

While recording, listen to your talent. Coach them, and make sure all their lines are being said with the right expressions. It's helpful to play the animation while their lines are recited.

Leave little pauses between each line. This will make your sound files easier to edit later.

Once you're finished a character's lines, stop recording. Use the rewind and play controls to preview the recording. Ensure it sounds the way you want. Save the recording and begin the next character's lines.

After the recording session, when the sound files you created are imported into your editing program, you'll be able to split the recordings into individual lines and place each line where it's needed, in relation to your animation.

Some will suggest recording all your characters' lines first, then animating to match the character's voices. Others suggest animating first, then recording dialog to match the animation. If you're animating characters with moving lips, you'll need to record the dialog first. Otherwise, it's your decision to make.

Preventing Plosives

Proper microphone placement can prevent common recording problems. Have you ever heard an audio recording that sounded like this?

"We have PHFFete on the scene, rePPHForting on the PHFFerfect... PUHF PUFH..."

These glitches called "plosives" result when a microphone is too close to the speaker. The "P" sound creates a gust of air, resulting in the bad audio.

To avoid this problem, keep the microphone a distance from the speaker, and point it at their chest, rather than their lips. Foam windscreens placed over the mic can also prevent plosive-explosions.

Music

More than any other sound element, music connects directly with our emotions. Music can transform daily life into a gripping adventure, or a short goodbye into a heartbreaking farewell.

Mac users have access to the GarageBand program in the iLife suite. It's a great resource for creating or recording music from scratch.

If you're making movies and showing them to a limited circle of family and friends, you can use CD tracks and downloaded music in your films. If you upload films with copyrighted music to the Internet, there is a chance the video will be removed, or the audio muted. Take time to research potential copyright and ownership issues if you choose to share your productions with a public audience.

Audio Editing with Audacity

After you've worked with audio for a while, you might want to create more complicated sounds. If so, you'll want to check out Audacity, a free open-source sound editing program. Audacity and similar programs allow you to record, edit, and enhance sounds by combining multiple sound tracks (download link at end of this chapter).

You can use Audacity's many effects to add an echo to your recordings, or raise the pitch of a sound higher or lower. You can remove audio glitches as well.

We'll use Audacity to record a voice, change the voice so it sounds like a chipmunk, and save the voice as a sound file that can be used in a movie.

First, plug your microphone into the computer, and move into a suitably quiet environment, away from noisy phone conversations, rampaging elephants, and the alien invasion taking place outside your window.

Repeat Last Effect   Ctrl+R
Amplify...
BassBoost...
Change Pitch...
Change Speed...
Change Tempo...
Compressor...
Echo...
Equalization...
Fade In
Fade Out
FFT Filter...
Invert
Noise Removal...
Normalize...
Nyquist Prompt...
Phaser...
Repeat...
Reverse
Wahwah...
Classic EQ(15)
Delay...
GVerb...
Hard Limiter...
High Pass Filter...
Low Pass Filter...
Notch Filter...
RFT-Vocoder
SC4...
Tremolo...

Audacity effects list (always growing!)

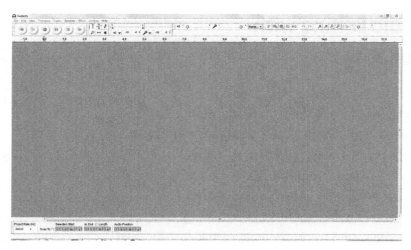

Start up Audacity. You'll see a window like this. Now, look at the upper left corner:

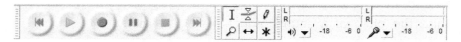

Familiarize yourself with these controls, because you'll be using them over and over again. If you forget what a button does, hover over the button with your mouse cursor, and a little reminder box will pop up.

Immediately to the right of the round control buttons, you'll see a collection of funny symbols. These are "tools" you'll use to manipulate and edit the audio in various ways.

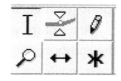

Also in the toolbar are two **audio meters**.

Audio meters show a little bar that jumps up and down as you record and play sound. The louder the sound is, the higher the bar jumps.

Recording Audio

Let's record a line of dialog. Make sure your microphone is plugged in. Hit the round red *Record* button. Say the following line:

"Hi, my name is Hammy the Hamster, and my voice sounds really squeaky. Hee hee hee!"

As you speak, you'll notice two things. First, the audio meter on the far right will be bouncing up and down. Secondly, a long blue squiggly line will appear in an audio track below the record button.

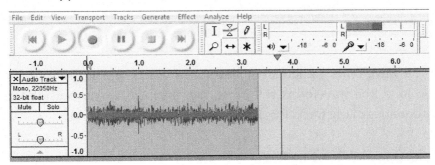

Note: If your microphone is plugged in, yet you do not see the audio meters jumping, and no sound is recorded, you'll need to select the correct audio input in Audacity's preferences. Click *Edit > Preferences* and in the *Recording* drop-down menu under *Devices*, click the *Microphone*, or *Line In* input.

When you finish saying your lines, hit the square *Stop* button. You've recorded your first sound! To play your recording back, hit the triangular *Play* button. If you really hate your recording, click the little **x** button next to **Audio Track**, and repeat the steps above until you have a recording you're happy with.

Let's go ahead and save our audio session. Click *File > Save Project...* and give the project a name, like "Hammy." If Audacity crashes, we'll have a backup of our recording. Keep saving as we move forward!

Let's edit this recording. You probably recorded a few seconds of silence before saying Hammy's lines. Let's trim this silence out of the clip.

Waveforms

Look at those blue squiggly lines again. These lines are called "Waveforms." The smaller these "waves" are, the quieter the sound is.

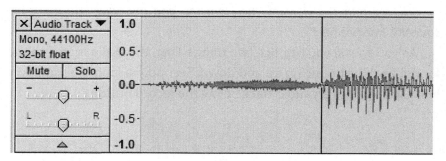

If the waveforms are loud, the waveforms will be big. If the sound is too loud, the waveforms will be so big, they clip, going outside the boundaries of the track. This isn't good.

Selecting and Deleting Audio

At the start of the track, you'll see a short section of very small waveforms. If you click **Play** and watch the track, you'll notice the sound is silent here. Let's remove this section.

In the tools area, click the tool that looks like a capitol **I**. Click the audio track, just after the small waveforms end (where the black line is above).

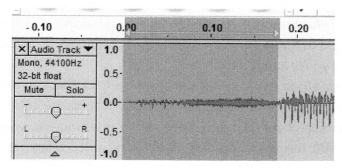

Backup!

If you want to back up an Audacity project to a hard drive, or CD, you'll have to copy two files, the project's .aup file, and associated data folder.

For example, our project has a project file, "Hammy.aup" and a file of audio data, "Hammy_data" that must be copied to your backup disk.

You'll notice a small vertical line has appeared where you clicked. If you hover over this line with your mouse, you'll notice the mouse cursor changing into a hand with a finger pointing left.

Click and hold the mouse button, dragging all the way back to the beginning of the recording, and release the mouse button. This will select all the audio up to the vertical line.

Alternatively, instead of clicking and dragging, you can click anywhere in the track and hit **Shift + J**. This will select all the audio from the beginning of the track to the vertical line.

To remove the selected audio, click **Edit > Delete**, or hit **Ctrl + K**. Zing! The audio is gone.

If you have a few seconds of silent audio at the end of your track too, you can remove it using the same method. Click and drag with the **I** tool until the end of the track, or click in one spot and hit **Ctrl + J** to select all the audio from the end of the track to the line.

You can also select and remove sections of audio in the middle of a recording by clicking and dragging anywhere in the track with the **I** tool. This is useful for removing unwanted pops, bumps, and rumbles.

If you're having trouble viewing all of the track at once, click the tool that looks like a magnifying glass, hold down the **Shift** key, and click the track. Zoom in by clicking the track with this tool, without holding down the **Shift** key.

Save your project. Let's go ahead and add the chipmunk effect to our voice.

Effect: Change Pitch

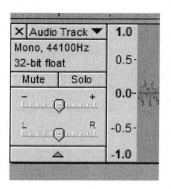

Click *Edit > Select > Select All*, or hit *Ctrl + A* to select the entire recording. Alternatively, you can click immediately below the words "Audio Track" to select the track.

Now, click *Effect > Change Pitch...*

If you've ever messed around with a cassette player, you may have figured out how to hit the fast-forward button so the tape played really fast, and everything sounded squeaky, like a chipmunk band.

If we changed the speed of our recording, the sound would play back faster, in a shorter amount of time. We don't want this. Instead of playing the sound faster, we're simply changing the pitch of the sound, so everything sounds higher.

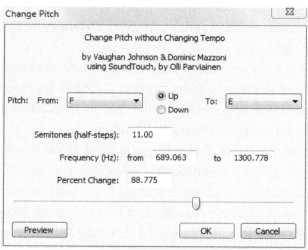

Here's the pitch effect window and parameters.

To change the pitch higher, grab the slider and drag it to the right. To change the pitch lower, drag to the left. To hear a sample of the effect, click *Preview*. When you're happy with the results, click *OK*.

Effect: Change Speed

If you really want to change the speed AND pitch of your recording, hit *Cancel* above, and click *Effect > Change Speed...* Drag the slider up and down, laughing hilariously at your goofy voice. Finally, click *OK*.

Saving a WAV File

We are done! Let's export an audio file that can be used in our movie projects.

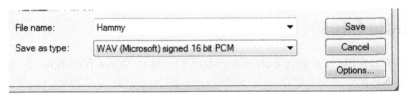

Click *File > Export...* You'll see a Save File dialog pop up. Give the file a name. In the *Save as Type* drop-down menu, click *"WAV (Microsoft) signed 16 bit PCM."* Click *Save*.

You may see another window pop up, asking you to label the file with some additional data. This is a useful way to organize your files. You

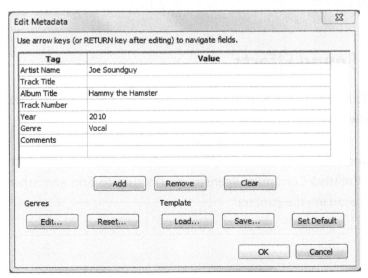

can see we've filled out the fields with some information pertaining to this recording. Click **OK** when you're done.

Congratulations! You've recorded, edited, and saved a line of dialog for your film. The process we've outlined above can be applied to any sound you record.

This chapter has just scratched the surface of the many things you can accomplish with Audacity. We encourage you to experiment with the program and its tools and effects.

Audio Files

The **Wave** file is a very common sound format. Wave files have a .WAV extension.

You may be able to create **MP3** or **WMA** files with your recording software. These formats were designed to reduce the size of audio recordings, making them easier to download and upload, with a slight loss in audio quality.

Your editing software should be able to use nearly any kind of sound file, but WAV files remain the most compatible.

Free Sound Effects

If you're looking for free, downloadable sound effects, create an account with **The Freesound Project:**

www.freesound.org/

Hundreds of sound hobbyists upload their creations to this site under Creative Commons licenses. You're sure to find something that can be used in your project!

Links

Go ahead and download the latest Beta version of Audacity. The beta is faster and has a better interface and more features than the current "stable" release. This chapter was written using the Beta version as a reference. The stable version's interface is different:

http://audacity.sourceforge.net/

Check It Out!

For a collection of free sound effects you can use in any project, visit:

StopmotionExplosion.com

Chapter 13

Files and Formats

So far, we've created basic movies and saved them to the computer. A little has been said about compressing movies with software called a **codec** that makes your movies easier to play and share.

There are many file formats and codecs. Each has its own advantages. This is a complicated subject. This chapter tries to explain everything in very simple terms.

There are three concepts to understand: **container formats**, image **compression**, and the **codec**.

Container Formats

Container formats are computer files, a type of computer "package." All kinds of containers exist. Filmmakers constantly use container formats holding video, images, and sounds.

If you have made animations with **SMA**, you have used the **AVI** container. AVI is a common video container. It can hold one track of video, and two tracks of audio.

If you have used MonkeyJam, you've used the **JPG** or **PNG** container. These containers hold still images.

If you've done some editing and added sound effects to a movie, you were probably working with **WAV** files, a common sound container. (A WAV file holds up to two tracks of audio and no video).

Container formats are almost always referred to as "files." You will hear references to "JPG files," "AVI files," "WAV files" and so on.

File Extensions

All files on the computer have an extension as part of their file name. When the computer looks at an extension, it knows what program should open the file.

Extensions always come after the file name.

- The file "Videoplayer.exe" has a **.exe** extension (it's a computer program).
- "Clip01.avi" has an **.avi** extension (it's a video file).
- "MyTextDocument.txt" has a **.txt** extension (it's a text file).

Extensions are usually invisible until you turn them on through your computer settings.

File Name   *Extension*

MyTextDocument.txt

Windows Extensions

On Windows computers, open your computer's Control Panel from the Start Menu, search for *Folder Options*, click the *View* tab, and uncheck *Hide extensions for known file types*. Click *OK*.

Mac Extensions

In OS X, click *Finder > Preferences* and under *Advanced*, check *Show all file extensions*.

Compression

When you create video files in SMA and set the compression settings to *Full Frames (uncompressed)*, the video is saved in an AVI container in a complete, unmodified state. The file contains the exact data captured.

The contents of a container format may be "compressed," and made smaller with the help of math formulas.

How does this work? Let's pretend we have some footage of the clear blue sky.

The uncompressed footage contains data for every point of color in the sky. Since the sky is blue, there are a lot of blue pixels with identical information in every frame. This redundant information makes the video file larger.

A compressed version of this footage will contain numbers specifying the color of blue, and the size and location of the area that it covers, instead of duplicating the blue pixels over and over in each frame. These formulas are much smaller than the pixels they replace, and make the video file smaller.

Compression formulas can be applied to video, sounds, and still images. A good compression formula can keep sound and video at near-uncompressed quality.

Codecs

Video and audio is compressed (or encoded) with something called a codec. The word "codec" is an acronym. It stands for:

COmpressor-DECompressor: **CODEC**

A codec is used to encode media. It is also used to decode media.

Codecs: Technical Explanation

When applied to a media file, a codec analyzes the content with various formulas, and decides how the file can be made smaller, usually by discarding data.

A process that discards information to make something smaller is described as **lossy** since information is being lost. A codec that does not discard data is described as **lossless**.

- Lossless codecs are used during capture and editing.
- Lossy codecs are used for sharing and distributing.

Lossy codecs *can* be used for editing, when computer power is limited, or image and sound quality isn't an issue.

Lossy compressed video looks blurred and blocky. Lossy audio sounds muddy, fuzzed, and tinny, like talking to someone on the phone. The more a file is compressed, the smaller it becomes, and the greater the loss of quality.

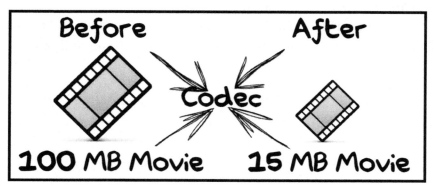

After a media file is compressed with a lossy codec, the original quality is gone. This is why you want to use video compressed with a lossless codec for capturing and editing if possible.

Repeatedly compressing video (once during capture, and once after editing) will result in unnecessary loss of quality, because data is discarded twice.

Codecs: Practical Explanation

A codec is a program you download, install, and it appears as a compression option in your video software. Computers usually have several dozen codecs installed by default.

Codec Issues

If video is compressed with a codec, moved to another computer, and opened. the video may not play until the correct codec is installed.

Hosting your video on a video sharing site is the best way for viewers to avoid these hassles. You the creator will need to compress and upload the video, which necessitates some knowledge of codecs and video formats.

We hope this section will clear some of the fog surrounding the subject.

Container Format List

Here is a handy guide to video formats and compression types. Know your extensions!

A brief summary:

- For maximum compatibility with older computers and operating systems, use the AVI or MEPG-1 format. If you're using AVI, apply a legacy codec.
- For maximum compression and quality, use MPEG-4, or the MOV and AVI formats with a MPEG-4 codec applied.

Type	File	Description Container Formats
DivX *(Format & codec. Codec can be applied to .AVI format)*	.divx	The .divx format is really an .AVI file compressed with the **Divx** codec. Continue on to the codec section for more information about DivX.
MPEG-4 *(Format)*	.mp4	MPEG-4 is an advanced video-audio compression algorithm that has its own container format. Most modern codecs and online video uses MPEG-4 technology for a high-quality image with a very small file size.
MPEG-1 *(Format)*	.mpg .mpeg	MPEG-1 has almost become a legacy format, but it has some advantages. Large file sizes, great picture quality. Simple MPEG converters can be downloaded on the internet.
Flash Video *(Format)*	.flv	The Flash Video format usually contains MPEG-4 encoded video. Video uploaded to video sharing websites, like YouTube is converted into FLV format. You can watch FLV video with the open-source **VLC Player**.

Container Formats

Type	File	Description
Audio-Video-Interleaved *(Format)*	.avi	Universally compatible. Many codec options. Works with any video player as long as the correct codec is installed.
Windows Media Video *(Format & codec. Codec can be applied to .AVI format)*	.wmv	WMV is widely used for Internet video distribution. Great compression! Non-Windows computers must download **Windows Media Player** before viewing this format.
QuickTime *(Format, & codecs)*	.mov	QuickTime is the .AVI format of the Mac world. A wide variety of codecs are "built in" to the format, eliminating pesky codec installations. QuickTime codecs cannot be applied to other formats, like the AVI format. **QuickTime Pro** ($$$) available on the Apple website, can be used for converting files into the QuickTime format.
DV *(Format & codec)*	.dv	You're unlikely to see the DV format until you begin using digital camcorders. DV is short for **Digital Video**. The DV codec is applied inside a video camera, as video is being written to tape. This video is transferred from the camcorder to the computer in the .dv format.

Codec List

Codecs can be divided into three groups.

Authoring

Authoring codecs are used during the capture and editing process. They compress the footage very slightly, preserving its original quality. Authoring codecs are also used for archiving purposes (backing your work up.)

Distribution

Distribution codecs are applied before the movie is distributed. The codec is applied during export from the editor, or afterwards; with a separate program.

Legacy

Legacy codecs have been around for a long time. They're found on nearly every computer. Most legacy formats are compatible with Apple, and the QuickTime player. Legacy video, with the exception of MPEG-1, compresses video poorly, with great loss of quality.

If a codec is not listed here, you're sure to find something about it online!

Windows Codecs

Name	Description
Windows Media 9 (WM9) *(Distribution codec)*	The codec used to compress **WMV** video can also be applied to AVI files.
DivX *(Distribution, MPEG-4)*	Back in the day, DivX had associations with movie piracy (arr!) but now enjoys a respected status in the filmmaking community. Download **DivX Free** from **DivX.com**. Download **XviD**, a DivX alternative, from **XviD.org**.
H.261, H.263 *(Legacy)*	Optimized for video conferencing. Works best with video that has little movement.
Cinepak codec by Radius *(Legacy)*	Cinepak is probably THE #1 most compatible AVI codec. Plays well on older computers. Encodes very slowly, with poor results.
DV *(Authoring)*	I mention DV again, because the DV codec can be applied to AVIs and the QuickTime format. Some programs may allow you to capture to the DV format as you animate.

Name	Description
M-JPEG (Authoring)	If you've ever surfed the web or worked with digital pictures, you've seen a JPEG image. Compresses each frame of video with JPEG compression. Lossless at 100%. No discernible loss at 85%.
PNG (Authoring)	Good for compressing RGB video. Lossless. Uses less space than the Animation codec.
None (Authoring)	None! Uncompressed RGB footage. Will chew through your free hard drive space very quickly.
Sorenson Video 3 (Legacy)	Sorenson was a commonly used QuickTime distribution codec. It has since been replaced by H.264 and MPEG-4.

QuickTime Codecs

Name	Description
MPEG-4 (Distribution)	MPEG-4 is a multimedia standard, delivering DVD-quality content to viewers. Most video sharing sites recommend compressing your video with this codec prior to uploading.
H.264 (Distribution)	Part of the MPEG-4 standard, this codec is commonly used for encoding and delivering HD video online.
DV (Authoring)	QuickTime can also encode with DV compression! Again, you'll probably use this if you're working with files from a DV camcorder.
Animation (Authoring)	Set at 100%, this codec is lossless. Compresses lines of the same color best. (Originally intended for cel-animation, but it works for stop motion too.)
Graphics (Authoring)	Intended for lossless compression of 8 bit graphics.

QuickTime Codecs

Compressing for the Web

People are becoming accustomed to high-quality Internet video, and more video sharing sites allow high-definition video uploads. Join the revolution and upload compressed, high resolution movies!

Let's look at recommended video specifications for YouTube uploads as of this writing.

Video

- **Resolution**: Original resolution. Upload your video with the same resolution it was captured in. This could be 640 x 480, or 320 x 240. YouTube has recently started accepting HD resolution uploads. These should be 1920 x 1080, or 1280 x 720.
- **Frame Rate**: Like your video resolution, this should be left the same as when captured.
- **Codec**: Choose a H.264 or MPEG-2 codec. Other codecs are acceptable, just make sure you have exported the video with the highest quality possible.
- **Video Containers**: FLV, MPEG-2 and MPEG-4. YouTube will accept AVI and WMV videos, but if you are trying to get the best YouTube video quality possible, use one of these recommended container format.

Audio

- **Codec**: If possible, choose an MP3 or ACC codec. Most video export dialogs will allow you to choose from a number of codecs. Nearly any will work, but the two above will keep sound quality high, and file size low.
- **Channels**: 2 (stereo audio)
- **Sampling rate**: 44.1kHz

These settings are typical for many video sharing sites. Following a website's recommended procedure for encoding video is the best way to improve the quality of your uploads.

Links

Quicktime
   http://www.apple.com/quicktime/download/
*Windows Media Video 9 (search for **wmv9VCMsetup.exe**)*
   http://www.microsoft.com/downloads
DivX
   http://www.divx.com/
FLV
   http://en.wikipedia.org/wiki/Flash_Video

Chapter 12

Video Editing

35mm film. Be happy you aren't using this stuff.

This chapter answers two frequently asked questions: "How do I put my video clips together?" and "How do I add sound to my movie?"

First, you'll learn some concepts and rules that every video editor should know. Then you'll have an opportunity to practice these rules, as you edit your first movie with a simple video editor.

Combining video clips, dialog, sound effects and music into a finished movie is the last step in the creative process.

Likely, some editing software came pre-installed with your computer. You'll find **Windows Movie Maker** on Windows XP, Windows Vista, and Windows 7 computers. **iMovie**, part of the iLife collection comes bundled with some installations of OS X.

iMovie

Mac only (sorry Windows users). **iMovie** has a wide selection of animated titles and transitions to choose from and can add effects such as falling rain and fog. The program also features two audio tracks. The latest version of iMovie can be purchased with the iLife suite.

The program is fun and easy to use and a highly recommended choice for beginning animators.

Windows Movie Maker

Windows Movie Maker 2.6 (WMM) is a simple video editor packaged with all installations of Windows XP, and Windows Vista. It does not come with Windows 7; however users can freely download the program from the Microsoft website

There are many tips and pointers in the program windows, making the learning curve fairly smooth. We also provide an in-depth introduction to WMM in this book.

Windows 7 users can download the **Windows Live** version of WMM as part of the Windows Live package; however the Live version lacks many great features.

The easiest way to find the older, better version of WMM on Microsoft's website is by googling "**Windows Movie Maker 2.6.**"

Other Programs

You can spend hundreds, even thousands of dollars on video editing software. **Adobe Premiere** is a popular video editor for Windows. Students with a valid ID, or homeschool organization membership can take advantage of Adobe's generous student discounts. Adobe's student license allows commercial work to be done with the software, useful if a day comes when you start getting paid to make movies.

The cheaper **Adobe Premiere Elements** is another option, though its features are limited.

Apple's **Final Cut** editor is offered in **Express** and **Pro** versions. **Final Cut Express** is cheaper and includes most of the Pro version's essential features

Sony Vegas is another popular choice. Vegas comes in several flavors, each with different features and prices.

While shopping for a video editor, look for the following features:

- Multiple audio and video tracks
- Compositing abilities, chroma-key (greenscreen) effects
- Video transitions
- Color correction tools
- Picture-in-picture effects, and the ability to rotoscope (draw on) video.
- The ability to import and export a multitude of video formats and resolutions, such as **AVI, HDV, DV, DV-AVI, MPEG-1/2/4, MPEG2-HD, DVD-Video, IFO/VOB, DivX, DivX HD, XviD, DVR-MS, TiVo, ASF, MOV, WMV, QuickTime, 3GP, MPEG2 Transport Stream, AVC (H.264), AVCHD.** You will be working primarily with AVI video files, but support for additional formats may be useful as you work on projects in the future.

Check It Out!

Download the sources and project file for a complete film, *Jack Spelt and the Sandstone Caves* at:

StopmotionExplosion.com

What is Editing?

Editing used to be a hands-on process. Real film was cut and glued (or "spliced") on an editing table and played back with special machines.

This changed when computers became powerful enough to edit video. Instead of gluing strips of film together, modern video editors work with a computer program that assembles meadia files into a movie. These programs are called Non-Linear Editors, often abbreviated as NLE.

Many of the terms used in a computer-based editing process are

taken from terms used by film editors. "Cuts" are literal scissor cuts used to remove "clips," short sections of the film roll. These clips were placed in a "bin" with other clips. Sometimes you hear a reference to a piece of footage or an idea ending up on the "cutting room floor," referring to a clip being tossed aside, swept up by the janitor and discarded.

When you sit down and prepare to edit, you are building on previous work. You have written a story, captured footage, recorded dialog, and most importantly, have a vision for the final result.

Working with 35mm film on an editing table back in the good ol' days, when editors were rockin' lab coats like mad scientists.

Editing Terms

NLE: Short for Non Linear Editor. Windows Movie Maker is one example.

Sources: Any file used in a movie project. Source files can be audio, video, pictures and graphics.

Project Files: Used by all NLE programs, sound programs and some animation programs. It's a file on the computer that links to your source files and remembers the order they appear in the movie.

Cuts: A term borrowed from film editing. A cut is where two separate pieces of film join, or two video files are divided and brought together.

Scenes: You can think of these as "chapters" in your movie's story. A scene can be made of many individual shots and camera angles, or just one.

Edward Dmytryk, (1908-1999) wrote a book titled: <u>On Film Editing</u>. In his book he lists seven rules which are very relevant for today's editors.

Rule 1: Never make a cut without a positive reason

If a shot captures emotion and action well, why show another? Cut only when absolutely necessary.

This rule does not imply that cuts are a bad thing. A cut is just another way to tell your story, and should be used strategically.

Rule 2: When undecided about the exact frame to cut on, cut long rather than short

This rule borrows from a carpentry principle. It's easier to saw boards long and trim them down, than too short and have to tack wood on the end. Cutting a strip of film too short requires gluing the film back together to find a better frame.

You don't have this problem when editing digital video. You can always click "Undo" and restore your work.

Rule 3: Whenever possible cut 'in movement'

Cuts can create the illusion that several cameras are on set and you're switching between them. In reality, there's one camera and a talented editor.

Cutting "in movement" helps this illusion. If a character's head is turning to look at something, cut to what they see in the middle of the turn. If someone jumps over a log, cut while they're flying through the air. Following this rule will make your cuts invisible to the viewer.

Rule 4: The 'fresh' is preferable to the 'stale'

If you display content that repeats established facts, or doesn't develop the story, your audience's attention will wander. They'll start noticing fingers creeping into the picture, or tape holding the set down. Keep things "fresh" with material that advances the story.

This rule is related to the third rule. Dead space between cuts will distract your audience, giving them time to concentrate on unimportant details.

Rule 5:   All scenes should begin and end with continuing action

If a scene begins with a boy pulling the cord of a lawnmower, the scene should end as he finishes mowing and reaches for the weedwhacker. He has successfully completed one action and is moving to the next.

Scenes should begin with action, and finish with the start of another action.

Rule 6: Cut for proper values rather than proper 'matches'

Continuity is the discipline of matching details between shots in a film. Since shots are usually filmed out-of-order, there's a high possibility of discrepancies between them.

For example, if a character drinks a glass of water, sets the empty glass down, and the next shot shows the same glass full of water, continuity is broken. This will confuse the audience.

Keeping continuity is not high on the editor's to-do list. These issues should be resolved during filming. If two shots don't match, you can try editing around it... but if you must choose between a poor shot with bad continuity, and a great shot with bad continuity, choose the great shot. Spielberg does so, you should too.

Rule 7: Substance first, then form

Dmytryk believed the editor's primary concern was improving the emotional power of the film's story, not following rules or set patterns. Editing is not a technical exercise, like math or science, but an art.

One of the best ways to learn the art of editing is by watching the work others have done, and asking questions about it. Why was the movie cut like this? What was the creator's intent? How could I apply these techniques in my work?

Editing Basics

This chapter will teach you basic NLE technique using **Windows Movie Maker 2.6**. Though this program lacks many features that high-end editing programs have, it's a great way to start learning basic skills that can be applied in any editing program you use.

Organization

Organizing resources you've gathered during the planning and shooting of your movie is important. You'll be more productive if you can find everything when it's needed!

Your resources might include animated video clips, photos, dialog you've recorded, sound effects, music, etc...

Give source files descriptive names, so you can find them later. Make new folders for each project and back up the folder frequently. It hurts to lose hours of hard work!

You'll also need a good collection of sound effects. If you arrange them in folders by subject, you'll have a valuable resource for your projects. Many free sounds can be found on the Internet. Higher quality sounds can be purchased and downloaded, or recorded yourself.

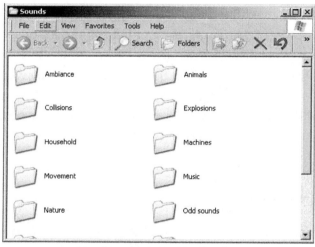

A well stocked sound collection.

Introduction to Windows Movie Maker

As you learn the features of Windows Movie Maker and start working with the program, remember two things:

- Most actions can be undone by clicking *Edit > Undo*. Remember this when you make a mistake!

- If you have a problem or question that's not answered here, tap into the community of WMM users on the Internet. Type "Windows Movie Maker" into any search engine, and a wealth of information will appear. Add a few words related to your

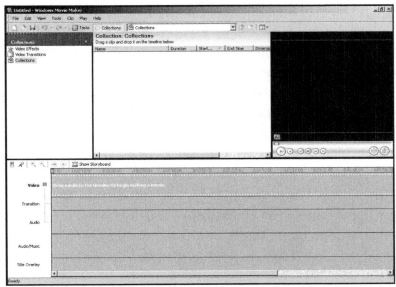

Windows Movie Maker 2.6 shortly after launching

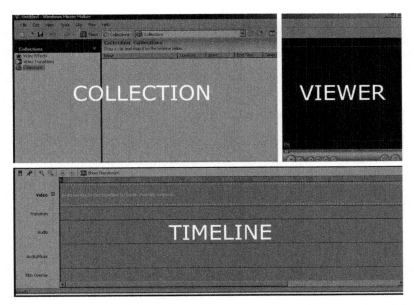

The three main areas of Windows Movie Maker. In this screenshot we've labeled them "Clip Collection," "Viewer," and "Timeline."

problem or a description of the error message (if any) to narrow down the results.

Let's begin! Start Windows Movie Maker (referred to as **WMM** from here on). It's usually found in the Windows Program Menu (click *Start*.)

If you cannot find the program, run a search, or visit the WMM directory: **C:/Program Files/Windows Movie Maker**

Windows 7 users can obtain the version of WMM used in this chapter by downloading *Windows Movie Maker 2.6* from the Microsoft website. A quick Google will reveal a download link.

To make WMM look like the illustration here, click the *Show Timeline* button in the bottom half of the screen, and display the Collections by clicking the *Collections* button at the top of the screen.

Up in the top left corner, click *File*, then *New Project*.

Clip Collection

This part of an NLE goes by many names, depending on the program you are using. "Clip Collection," "Clip Panel," and "Browser" are a few. The collection is where source files are placed before they are used in the

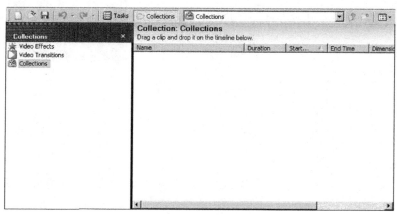

The Clip Collection

project. It's like a box for your files, holding them until they are dragged onto the "timeline" for editing.

The work of moving sources into the Collection is called "Importing." Importing is the first step to creating a movie in an NLE. WMM's import process can be annoying, but the kinks are easy to work around. Let's import a few sources right now!

Click **Tools** at the top of the screen, then, in the drop-down menu that appears, click **New Collection Folder**. Name the folder something appropriate by going to the top of the screen, clicking **Edit**, then **Rename**. Great! We're all set to import some sources.

Importing Video

In Windows Movie Maker, you import files by clicking **File** in the upper left corner, then **Import into Collections...** or by clicking **Import Media Items**. A file dialog comes up.

Navigate around the computer until you find one of your video files. Click the file to select it, then hit the **Import** button. If you have many

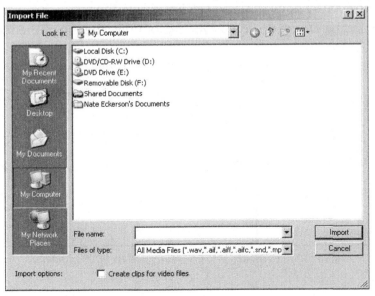

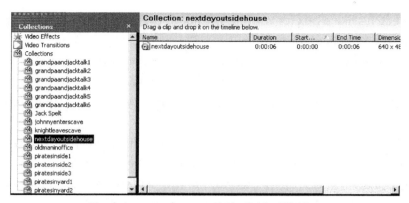

Newly imported sources in individual folders

video files to import, you can select several at once, by holding the *Ctrl* key down and clicking each file. When finished, click *Import*.

In some versions of WMM, after importing a bunch of video sources, you have a collection folder for every imported clip.

It's better to have all the clips in one folder. Fortunately, you can drag the movie sources out of their individual folders, into the one we created earlier.

Once you've done this, you can just delete the empty folders. Click them and hit *Delete* on your keyboard, or up at the top of the screen, click *Edit > Delete*.

All the sources moved into one folder. Delete empty folders.

Importing Sound

Let's import some sound files. Click on the movie's collection folder and again, click: *File > Import Into Collections...* Navigate to your sound folder and start importing every sound you think the film will require. Car sounds, people sounds, water sounds, explosions, anything. WMM doesn't create separate folders for sound sources, so there's nothing to delete this time.

Missing Sources

Importing is only *telling* the NLE where source files are on your computer. Sources are *not moved or copied*, only linked to, or referenced. If you move or delete sources on the hard drive, the missing source files will look like little red X's in the viewer:

Name	Duration	Start...	End Time	Dimensi
✖ Clip (4)	0:00:14	0:00:00	0:00:14	640 x 4
✖ Clip (5)	0:00:03	0:00:00	0:00:03	640 x 4

Lost source files!

Double-clicking a missing source brings up a file dialog, allowing you to locate the original file, which hopefully has been moved, and NOT deleted! If it's gone you'll need your backup. You have a backup, right?

Backup!

You should back up the project file too, along with your sources. By doing so, you can re-construct your movie if anything happens. Windows Movie Maker project files have the **.mswmm** extension.

More Organization

Earlier in the chapter we mentioned how important organization is. Looking at this screenshot, you can see how we've arranged the video and audio sources in separate folders.

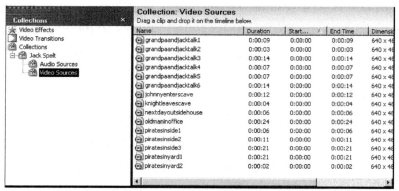

It's good practice to separate your video and audio into separate folders

You can make these "folders-within-folders" by right-clicking the movie's collection folder, and selecting "New Collection Folder"

You've done a lot of work! It's time to save the project. Click *File > Save Project*, and give the project a name. Then click the *Save* button. Save frequently! If the unthinkable happens, you'll feel much better if you've only lost 5 minutes of work.

Important Tip: You've probably noticed these two things in the

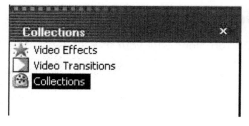

Collection: "Video Effects," and "Video Transitions." These folders contain special effects and transitions, which can be applied to video clips placed on the second part of the WMM editor, the Timeline.

Timeline

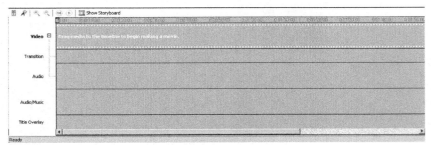

The Timeline!

The timeline looks a little like a ruler, except it measures time instead of inches. First, notice how the timeline is divided by several horizontal lines. These spaces are called "tracks." If you look on the left side, you'll

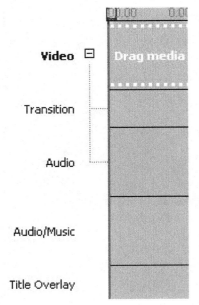

see each track is labeled. There's a "Video" track (with two subtracks: "Audio" and "Transition" which we'll explain later). There's also an "Audio" track, and a "Title Overlay" track.

Not surprisingly, video sources are placed on the "Video" track, and audio sources on the "Audio" track.

Adding Video to the Timeline

We're ready to start putting the movie together! Go into the Collection folder and find the video source that appears first in your movie. Click and drag it down to the "Video" track. See how the cursor changes when you're over the timeline? Release the mouse button to place the first source.

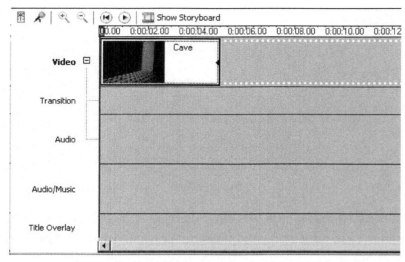

First video source added to the timeline.

Continue dragging video clips down to the timeline, in the order you want them to appear. Now play everything by clicking the **Play** button on the timeline

The zoom buttons look like magnifying glasses

If you've followed these instructions correctly, your video clips should play back in perfect order in the Viewer. Congratulations! You've taken another step towards completing your movie!

If you've added many sources to the timeline, you'll soon get tired of scrolling back and forth to see them all. By clicking the **Zoom In** and **Zoom Out** buttons on the timeline, you can see more of the timeline at once. Pressing **F9** zooms to the point where everything in the timeline is visible.

The play button looks like a little arrow pointing right. The rewind button is next to it.

To the right of **Zoom In** and **Zoom Out** are two buttons that play and rewind the timeline. You've already clicked **Play**. Click the left-pointing arrow next to **Zoom Out** to rewind the timeline.

Adding Audio to the Timeline

Now that the movie has some video, it's time to add sound. Audio sources are added to the timeline exactly like video sources.

Look in the Collection folder, and find the first sound you want in the movie. Drag it down onto the "Audio" track in the timeline.

You probably noticed you couldn't drag the sound onto the first audio track, only the one underneath it. The first track is for audio contained in video clips.

This is a shortcoming of WMM. After you've placed a few more audio clips on the timeline, you'll find yourself wishing for another track of audio. We'll explain a workaround for this later. For now, press the **Play** button.

The movie will play, and you will hear the sound! Chances are the sound is not in the right place. Stop and rewind the movie, then click and drag the sound clip along the track, until it's roughly where you want it.

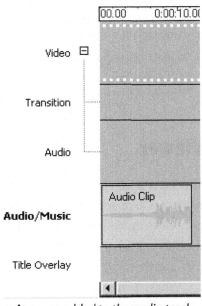

A source added to the audio track

Continue playing and tweaking the sound's position, until it's exactly where it needs to be.

WMM allows sounds to be "stacked." They may be stacked two high, by dragging them on top of each other. This is not a perfect solution because the sounds fade in and out, but if you have several short sounds, this is a handy way to blend them together.

To overcome WMM's one audio track limitation, you can fill the audio track with clips, export the entire movie using a high-quality setting, import the movie back into WMM and continue adding sounds. We'll explain the export process later in this chapter.

Let's discuss the Viewer next, before editing the rest of our movie. The viewer and timeline work closely together. It's hard to use one without knowing how the other works.

Troubleshooting

If the video does not play back smoothly, but stutters and jerks, skipping frames and sections of video, this is a symptom of not compressing your video before editing.

Page to the VirtualDub chapter at the end of this book for video compression instructions.

Viewer

The viewer is like a TV screen with a DVD player attached. The movie project you're editing is the DVD. You can play the project by clicking the play button. You stop playback by clicking stop, and pause the project by clicking pause. When you play, pause, rewind or fast forward, you're moving through *time*.

When a movie is rewound all the way to the beginning, you're starting at 0:00:00.00. **Zero** hours, **zero** minutes, **zero** seconds.

The Viewer

If you push play, and pause 30 seconds later, you've moved ahead to 0:00:30.00. **Zero** hours, **zero** minutes, **30.00** seconds. If you rewind 10 seconds, you're at 0:00:20.00. **Zero** hours, **zero** minutes, **20.00** seconds.

In the viewer, click the play button again. Notice two things. First, in the viewer, two times are displayed.

The time on the left shows how much time the sources in the project add up to, the *length* of the project. This could be anywhere from no time at all, up to 4 hours. Current time is displayed on the right. The current time is where the playhead rests on the timeline.

Click the *Play* button once more. This time, look at the timeline. See that vertical line moving along?

This is the playhead. It marks the current playing time, and can be used for many other things. Try this!

Move the mouse to the top of the timeline, so the cursor rests over the ruler measuring time. A vertical line will appear under the cursor, with a little box next to it, showing what time you're pointing at. Move the cursor back and forth. See the time change?

The black bar displays the "time" you're pointing at...

Move the cursor along the "ruler" somewhere in the middle of the sources you've placed, and click the mouse.

The playhead jumps to the time you clicked. Look at the viewer. You've advanced to the middle of the movie, without touching fast-forward or rewind! Now, try clicking the little square on the top of the playhead, and dragging it along the ruler (watch the viewer as you do this).

You are rewinding and fast forwarding through the movie by dragging the playhead around. This technique is called "scrubbing," and is very handy for quickly moving to a place in the project.

You might be tempted to do all of your rewinding and fast forwarding this way, but the playback buttons in the viewer are very handy too. In particular, the **Previous Frame** and **Next Frame** buttons let you move the playhead very precisely, one frame at a time.

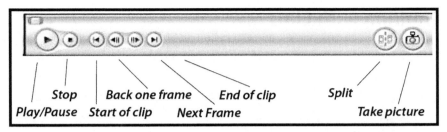

These buttons work somewhat like the controls on a DVD player remote. Depending on your version of WMM, not all of the buttons pictured may be visible.

Look at this picture for a quick reference for the buttons in the viewer.

- *PLAY*: Starts playing the movie from the playhead's position (changes to PAUSE when clicked). Hitting the space bar also plays and pauses your movie.
- *STOP*: Stops playback, and rewinds (moves playhead) to the beginning of the project.
- *BACK*: Moves playhead to beginning of clip.
- *PREVIOUS FRAME*: Rewinds one frame. Hold down to rewind.
- *NEXT FRAME*: Moves forward one frame. Hold down to fast-forward.
- *NEXT*: Moves playhead to end of clip (or beginning of next clip).

In addition to these navigational buttons are two with editing functions: *Take Picture*, and *Split Clip*. We'll cover their uses in the next section of this chapter.

All these buttons are also accessible from the *Play* menu, or *Tools > Take Picture from Preview*. Also note, all buttons pictured may not be visible in some versions of WMM.

Working with Clips

Let's keep editing the movie. Add any remaining video sources, and a few essential sounds to the timeline. Try to place sources roughly where they belong.

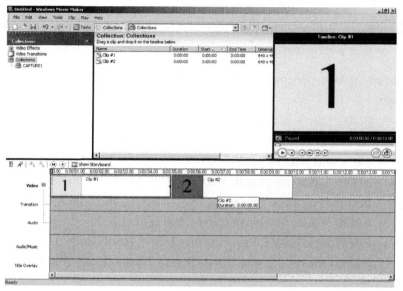

Two clips: Clip #1 and Clip #2 have been added to the timeline

If you accidentally mess up and place a wrong source on the timeline, then click the source, select *Edit > Delete*, and try again. Remember, you're not deleting anything on the computer! You're only removing the source from the timeline. Clicking *Edit > Undo* is another way to fix the mistake (hit **Ctrl+Z**).

If you want to drop a source between two clips on the timeline, simply drag and drop the source where the two clips meet. If the source is already on the timeline, you can shuffle clips around and arrange them in a different order by dragging and dropping. Don't forget, you can zoom in and out to see more of the timeline.

If you try to drag a clip backwards onto another clip, you'll notice a funny blue wedge appearing on the clip that's not moving.

This is a transition in the making. If you dropped the clip right now, and played the movie, you'd see the first clip fade away, and the second one appear underneath it. We'll explain transitions later in this chapter. Continue dragging the clip until the wedge disappears, and release the mouse button. The clip should drop into place.

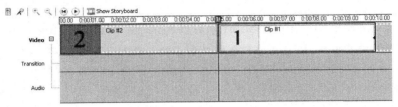

Clip #2 has been dragged and dropped in front of Clip #1

Trimming and Splitting

Sometimes you want to trim a little extra off a clip and make it shorter. Or, several scenes may be contained in one clip, and you want to separate them. This is where trimming and splitting are very handy.

First, select the clip by clicking. Move the mouse to one end of the clip.

You'll see the mouse cursor change into a box with two arrows. Click and drag the mouse towards the beginning of the clip to trim the clip down to size.

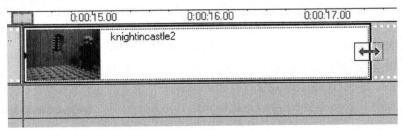

This clip needs to be shortened

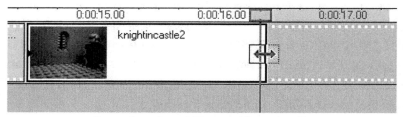

Removing about 3/4 second from the clip

If you trim the clip too short, you can drag it back to its full length.

While you're dragging the end of the clip, the viewer shows what frame you're trimming to. To trim in smaller increments, zoom in on the clip.

Splitting

Cuts are typically made by chopping, or "splitting" a source into smaller clips. You split a source into pieces, and insert clips between them.

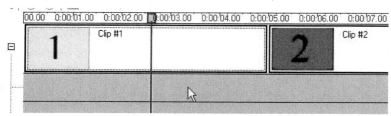

Preparing to split a clip

Move the playhead where you want the split to occur. Don't forget: the viewer's **Next Frame** and **Previous Frame** buttons let you move the playhead one frame at a time. Once the playhead is sitting on the frame where you want the split to happen, click the **Split** button in the viewer.

Snip! The source has been split into two parts.

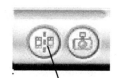

The Split button

Each half is an individual clip. The clips can be moved, trimmed, and split again if you wish.

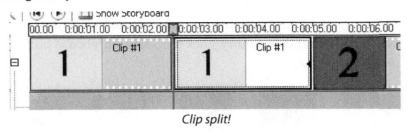

Clip split!

Copying and Pasting

Clips can be copied, cut, and pasted, just like you were working with text. Select a clip by clicking, and go to **Edit > Copy**.

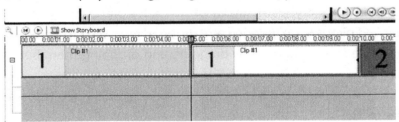

Clip #1 has been copied and pasted

Clips are pasted at the playhead, so before you paste, drag the playhead where you want the clip, and click **Edit > Paste**.

When you're pasting, the playhead's position is very important. If you paste when the playhead is on top of another clip, the pasted clip is inserted right in the middle. This is a great technique for inserting cuts.

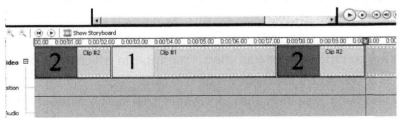

Clip #2 is split by pasting Clip #1 on top of it

Storyboard

This is a different way to arrange video sources on the timeline. It's not as powerful as the timeline method, but it's simple, and a great way to throw sources together in a hurry. Click the *Show Storyboard* button on the timeline.

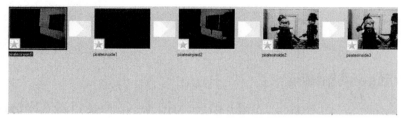

The Storyboard view

This is the "storyboard" layout of WMM. It's pretty straightforward. Video and pictures are dragged and dropped onto the big squares. You can shuffle sources around by dragging and dropping them between squares.

Storyboard view is a handy way to add and edit video **transitions** and **effects**.

Transitions

A transition is an artistic, visual way to move between two clips. A transition can be used to show the passage of time, to soften an abrupt cut, or show a change in location.

The most common and flexible transition is the Dissolve. Sometimes Dissolve is called a "Crossfade," or "Mix." WMM calls the dissolve a "Fade" which is incorrect. A fade is a transition between solid color and video. Another commonly used transition is the Wipe, in which a line or shape makes a moving boundary between two clips.

Everything else falls into the effect transitions category. Effect transitions can look like anything; from pages turning to flying cows.

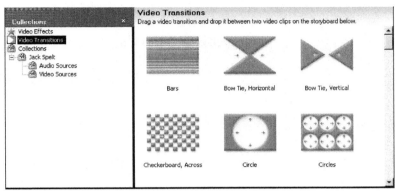

Bars, Bowties and Checkerboards

WMM comes with a wide variety, which you can preview by clicking **Transitions** in the Collections folder.

Clicking a transition loads a preview into the viewer, which you can play to see what it looks like.

Adding a transition is simple. In the timeline, pick a video source, and start dragging it backwards, on top of the one before it.

A blue wedge begins forming, and a box appears next to the cursor, showing how far the clip has been dragged. Release the clip after its slid back about a second

Handy Hint

It may be tempting to fill a movie with wacky transitions, but it's more filmic to use only cuts, dissolves and wipes.

Save effect transitions for those really special projects... like used car commercials.

Hit *Play* to see the transition. The first clip "dissolves," and the second appears underneath it.

You'll notice a box labeled "Fade" has appeared. This is a Transition track. The box is labeled "Fade," because this is the kind of transition being used. Remember the transitions we were looking at earlier? By

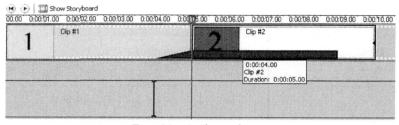

Transition in the making...

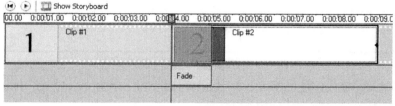

Cross fade transition completed

dragging and dropping transitions on this box, the type of transition can be changed. Try it!

It's simpler to add transitions in the storyboard view, and fine-tune them in the timeline. To add transitions in the storyboard, simply drag and drop them on top of the smaller boxes. A 1.25 second transition will be added between the clips. (*1.25* seconds is the default length. This can be changed under *Tools > Options*.)

Transitions are removed the same way sources are. Select and delete them.

Effects

Return to the timeline view (if you haven't already), go to the Collections folder, and click *Effects*.

Many interesting effects appear. All of them can be previewed in the viewer by double-clicking.

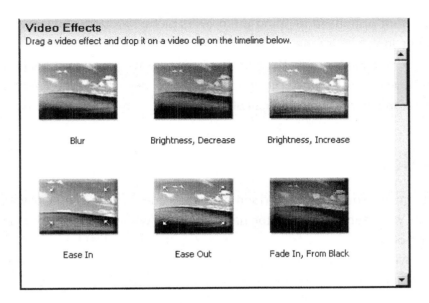

Choose an interesting effect. Drag and drop it on top of a clip in the timeline. (You do the same thing in storyboard view; simply drag and drop an effect onto a video square).

A star appears on the clip. This shows an effect has been applied. Play the movie to see the result of your effect.

Several effects are particularly useful, including Fade In/Fade Out, Ease in/Ease Out, and

Check It Out!

The "Sepia" and "Film Age, Old" effects were applied to the opening of Jack Spelt. This suggests the events happened a long time ago.

different options for flipping the movie's picture around. Making your video look "old" is fun.

If you apply several effects to a clip, chances are you'll want to remove some. By right-clicking the clip and selecting *Video Effects...* you can remove some of, or all of, the effects.

Titles

Eventually you'll want to add some opening titles, with the name of your film, your studio logo, and the names of those who made it all possible. And of course you need rolling credits for the end of the film.

WMM has a very simple interface for creating titles and credits. Open this interface by clicking *Tools > Titles and Credits...*

Click *Add title at the beginning of the movie.*

There's two areas for type. The top box is for the main title. Any text added here is displayed in big bold letters. The bottom box is for a smaller sub-title.

Type something like: "My Amazing Movie" in the top box, and "It's the Best!" in the bottom. Look at the viewer.

The text is displayed in the viewer as you type. After you finish, the text is automatically animated.

Where do you want to add a title?

Add <u>title at the beginning</u> of the movie.

Add <u>title before the selected clip</u> in the timeline.

Add <u>title on the selected clip</u> in the timeline.

Add <u>title after the selected clip</u> in the timeline.

Add <u>credits at the end</u> of the movie.

<u>Cancel</u>

Title and Credits tool

WMM comes with many different title animations, and allows you to change the color and type of text. These options can be accessed by clicking *Change the title animation*, and *Change the text font and color*.

When you're finished, click *Done, add title to movie*, and a new title clip appears on the timeline!

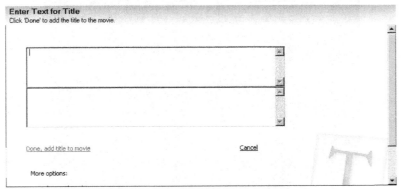

Add the main and secondary titles here

Adding credits is done the same way, except there are more fields to fill in. Click **Tools > Titles and Credits...** then **Add credits at the end of the movie**. Once you're finished, you can change the color and animation by clicking **Change the title animation**, and **Change the text font and color**.

After titles and credits have been placed on the timeline, they can be adjusted to any length you desire. Using the previously described method for trimming, click and drag the title clip's ends. When you play the clip again, you'll notice the titles are moving a lot slower, or a lot faster, depending whether you made the clip longer or shorter.

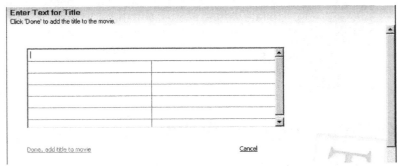

Credits. Add names on the lines.

A new title. Click the play button to see it fade in and out.

Keep your titles short as possible. The shorter your film is, the shorter your titles should be.

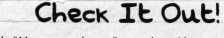

Check It Out!

A title *"Many years later..."* was placed between the pirate writing a letter, and the old man looking at the map. You can use a title to set the time and place, like, *"Paris 1789."*

Recording Sound and Dialog

WMM includes a handy sound recording tool. It's useful for recording character dialog, because the video plays while you record, and the recorded clip is placed directly on the timeline. Open the recorder window by clicking **Tools > Narrate Timeline...**

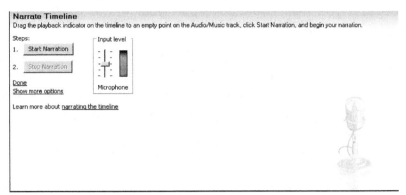

The Narrate Timeline tool

This is another simple interface that needs very little explanation. Click **Start Narration** to begin recording sound. When you're finished, click **Stop Narration**. A save file dialog will pop up. Name the sound and save the file. It will automatically be imported and placed on the timeline, at the playhead's current position.

A little note. The playhead must be moved to a point in the timeline where there's no sound, or the record button will be grayed out.

Sharing Your Movie!

It's time to package the project into one movie file that others can share, download, and watch on their computer! In WMM, the process begins by clicking **File > Save Movie File...** or **Publish Movie...**

A list of options comes up. Now it's time to think. Exporting a video file is always a trade-off between quality and file size. Do you want your video to have a high-quality picture, and crisp audio? Or can you settle for a lower-quality version that is easier to transfer over the Internet?

Fortunately, WMM has lots of export settings for different situations.

You can export movie files optimized for e-mail, CDs, the Internet, and playing back on your own computer.

Because you really want to export your movie NOW, click *My Computer*, then *Next*.

A window appears. Choose a name for the movie file, and decide where it will be saved on the computer. You should make a special folder for your finished movies, but if you're in a hurry, it's OK to save them on your desktop. Type a name for your movie file and click *Next*.

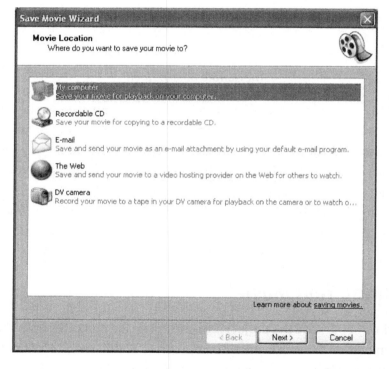

Tweaking settings to achieve the best picture with the smallest file size is a fine art! You could go with what the wizard has suggested–a relatively small, low quality movie. If you click *Show more choices...* and *Other Settings*, many different options appear.

Most of the settings are arranged by Internet connection speeds.

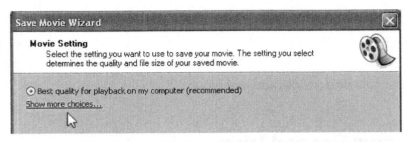

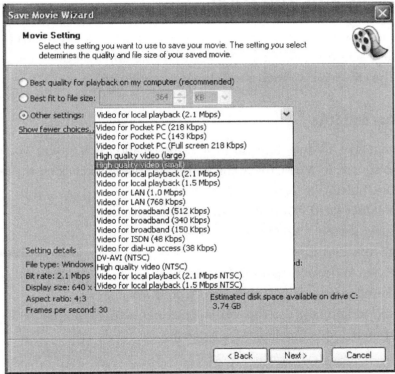

This is helpful when you're e-mailing the movie file, or making it available for download. It's a good idea to export your movie with the best possible quality settings, especially if you're uploading the video to a sharing site, like YouTube. The website will re-encode the video, so it's best to upload high-quality material.

The movie will begin exporting. Depending on the length of the movie and your computer's processing power, it may take minutes, or even hours. You could jump around the room impatiently waiting for the export to finish, or you could read the next section with some additional editing tricks and techniques!

Editing: Tips and Tricks

An animator can get away with some sneaky dodges that wouldn't work in a live action movie. Many of these tricks are applied during the edit, but they must be planned ahead while you animate.

Photos and Stills

You can take a single frame from your movie and use it as you would a video source. In WMM, these still frames are made by clicking the take picture button, located in the viewer, or clicking *Tools > Take Picture from Preview.* After you save this "picture" (frame), WMM will automatically import it into the Clip Collection. Frames are kept in the collection folder until placed on the timeline.

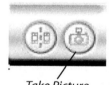

Take Picture

If used carefully, this technique can produce great results. Additionally, you can take still pictures with a digital camera and insert them in the timeline like a video file.

Live Video Capture

For scenes that require falling, traveling, exploding, or camera movement that would be difficult to animate, this technique's simplicity can't be beat.

Note: The capture tool is not available with all installations of WMM.

Make sure your camera is plugged into the computer. Start Windows Movie Maker, and open or create a project. WMM's live capture tool is accessed by clicking *File > Capture Video*.

The camera should be selected. Note the *Configure...* button.

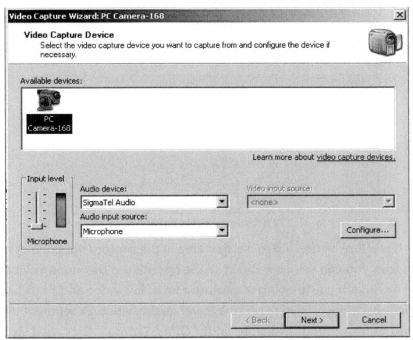

Capture video!

Clicking this lets you configure the camera and video settings.

It's best to work with the highest quality sources possible. If your computer is capable, capture footage at *640 x 480*, with as little compression as possible.

When everything is configured, click *Next*, and in the window that appears, type a name and select a location for the video file. Click *Next* again, when you're finished.

The next window determines how compressed the captured video is. You've already seen something like this if you exported a movie file in WMM.

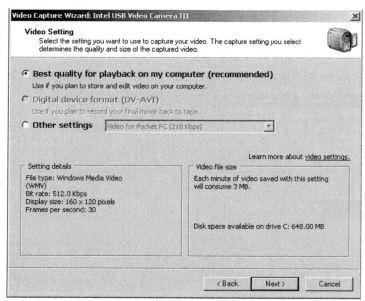

Choose your video quality

If you look at the "Video file size" area in the bottom right half of the window, you can see how much space per minute the video will take on the drive. If you're going to capture a lot of live video and don't have much space, you'll have to capture lower quality video. Experiment with some of the settings available under *Other Settings*. Click *Next* when finished.

Finally, you're ready to capture. Click *Start Capture* to start, and *Stop Capture* to stop. The preview window will show what's being captured. To the left, you can see how much video has been captured, and how big the video file is getting. Click *Finish* when you're done. The file will be imported into the collection, and you can add it to the timeline.

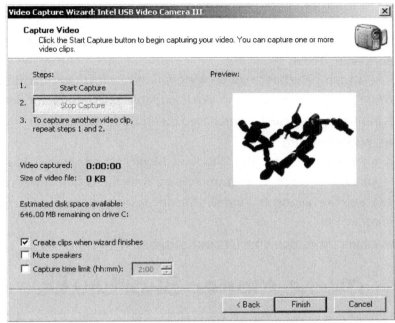

Ready to capture

Movie Maker Resources

A thriving Internet community has sprung up around Windows Movie Maker. Here are two websites you should visit. Both contain a wealth of information about the program!

www.papajohn.org

www.windowsmoviemakers.net

More Effects

Eventually you may become bored with the effects, transitions, and titles that WMM is packaged with. Good news is, more are available. The "Windows Movie Maker 2 Creativity Fun Pack" with titles, sounds, and music is available in the "Windows XP PowerToys and Add-ins" section of the Microsoft website. You can search the site for it, or type the following address into your browser:

http://www.microsoft.com/windowsxp/downloads/powertoys/ mmcreate.mspx

The Pixelan company has created a wide variety of effects and transitions for WMM. They are available in downloadable packs for a moderate price. Multiple packs can be purchased for additional savings:

www.Pixelan.com

Many effects come free! The Windows Movie Makers forum has an entire section devoted to custom effects, transitions, and titles. Visit this site, and the Microsoft Windows Movie Maker newsgroups for more information:

www.windowsmoviemakers.net/forums

Movie Maker Shortcuts

Following is a list of common WMM tasks, and keyboard shortcuts for each. Learn how to edit with one hand on the mouse, the other on your keyboard. You'll work faster, and more efficiently.

Links

Adobe Software
http://www.adobe.com/
Final Cut
http://www.apple.com/finalcutstudio/
www.apple.com/finalcutexpress
Sony Vegas
http://www.sonycreativesoftware.com/vegassoftware

Function   Shortcut

Open project . . . . *CTRL+O*

Save project . . . . *CTRL+S*

Export movie . . . . *CTRL+P*

Capture live video from camera . . . . *CTRL+R*

Import source file . . . . *CTRL+I*

Undo last action . . . . *CTRL+Z*

Redo last action . . . . *CTRL+Y*

Cut . . . . *CTRL+X*

Copy . . . . *CTRL+C*

Paste . . . . *CTRL+V*

Delete . . . . *DELETE*

Select all clips . . . . *CTRL+A*

Rename collection or clip *F2*

Clear the timeline . . . . *CTRL+DELETE*

Switch storyboard/timeline view . . . . *CTRL+T*

Zoom in on the timeline . . . . *PAGE DOWN*

Zoom out on the timeline . . . . *PAGE UP*

Add selected clips to the timeline . . . . *CTRL+D*

Preview project in full screen . . . . *ALT+ENTER*

Set start trim point . . . . *CTRL+SHIFT+I*

Set end trim point . . . . *CTRL+SHIFT+O*

Clear trim points . . . . *CTRL+SHIFT+DELETE*

Split a clip . . . . *CTRL+L*

Combine contiguous clips . . . . *CTRL+M*

Nudge clip left . . . . *CTRL+SHIFT+B*

Nudge clip right . . . . *CTRL+SHIFT+N*

Play and Pause . . . . *SPACE*

Playhead Right . . . . *ALT+RIGHT ARROW*

Playhead Left . . . . *ALT+LEFT ARROW*

Chapter 14

VirtualDub

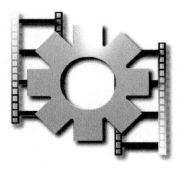

VirtualDub is a powerful video processing and capture tool. It's free to download, under the "GNU General Public License" (GPL).

VirtualDub comes in several flavors. In this chapter, you'll learn how to use **VirtualDubMod**. VirtualDubMod has all the functionality of the original program, with a few added features. You can also use the original Virtual Dub to complete the tutorials (download links at the end of the chapter).

VirtualDubMod's primary usefulness for animators is the program's ability to disassemble a video file into individual pictures, and assemble a series of pictures into a video file.

You'll explore the program's interface, compress a video file into a smaller size, and learn how to convert a series of pictures into video (and vise versa).

After you start the program for the first time, a few windows will pop up, explaining the GPL license, and some features of VirtualDubMod. After you've clicked OK several times, the main window appears.

If you read the chapter on editing, you'll notice some similarities between VirtualDubMod and Windows Movie Maker. Files are imported (brought into the program) modified in some way, and exported (output from the program in a new form).

VirtualDub ready to go!

VirtualDubMod has a simple timeline and playhead, the ability to delete single frames, or sections of video, buttons for playing, rewinding, moving frame-by-frame, and even some effects! VirtualDubMod calls effects "filters."

The great thing about VirtualDubMod is its simplicity. Compressing and converting a video file can be completed a few clicks!

Compressing a File

Let's return to video compression. First, we must import a file to work with. In the top left corner of the screen, click *File > Open Video File...*

In this example, we're compressing an uncompressed animation we made in SMA. When we're done, the video file will take up much less space on the disk, and be easier to edit in Windows Movie Maker.

This file window has some unusual options in the lower left corner. We'll come back to the two checkboxes in the next section. Select your video file by clicking it, then click the *Open* button.

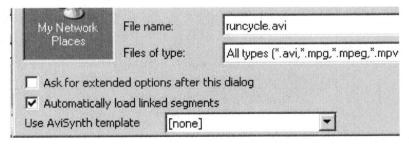

The video appears in VirtualDubMod! You can scrub through the video by dragging the bar in the slider back and forth. (If you read the editing chapter, you'll notice this bar acts as the playhead). Experiment with the navigation buttons: *Play, Rewind, Goto End*, etc.

Now, set the compression for your output video. Click *Video > Compression...*

Depending which codecs you have installed, this list might be very long, or very short. What codec you choose depends on the finished file's purpose. For the best compatibility with Windows Movie Maker, use the **Microsoft Windows Media Video 9** codec.

Save a compressed video file! Click *File > Save As...* name the video file, and click *Save*. Done! Your file is compressed.

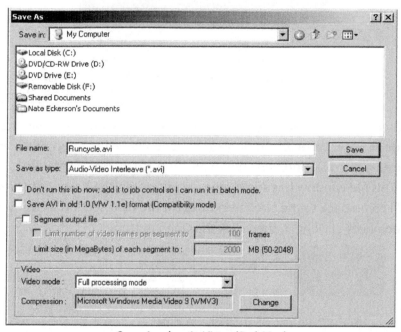

Save As... box in VirtualDubMod

Converting Pictures into Video

This is the section you need to read if you're following the **Flight** and **Paint.NET Blaster** tutorials. Whether you're animating with a digital still camera and need to assemble your photos into a video file, or want to convert video into pictures for editing with a paint program, VirtualDubMod is an excellent tool for the job.

If you're converting a series of pictures, you should make them a numbered sequence, by naming them like this: *Picture000, Picture001,*

Picture002, Picture003, and so on. VirtualDubMod can automatically import every file in a numbered sequence (saves a LOT of clicking!)

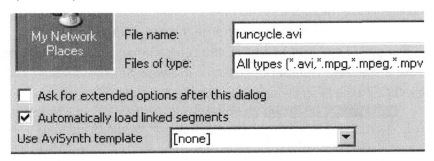

After clicking *File > Open video file...* make sure the *Automatically load linked segments* box in the lower left corner is checked. Select the first picture in the numbered sequence and click *Open*. The numbered files will appear in VirtualDubMod.

Now the pictures must be resized—shrunk into video dimensions. If you know the pictures are already the correct resolution, skip this step.

Resize the pictures

Otherwise, continue reading. Resizing is done with a **filter**. Click **Video > Filters...** Click the **Add** button. The following window appears: Find the "resize" filter. Select this filter by clicking, and click **OK**. Another window will pop up, letting you choose the new width and height.

A width of 640 and height of 480 is recommended, if you plan to create a standard resolution video for the web. Set these values and click **OK**. Exit the Filters window by clicking **OK**.

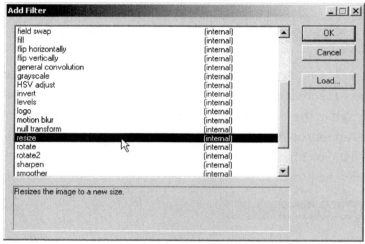

The VirtualDub filters

The resize filter has been applied! There's plenty of neat filters in VirtualDubMod. Try experimenting with them sometime!

Before saving the pictures as a video file, make sure the frame rate is set correctly, by clicking **Video > Frame rate...** Change it to the correct speed. (If you animated at **15** frames per second, the frame rate should be 15). Click **OK**.

Set the compression, (click **Video > Compression**), and create the video (click **File > Save as...** type name, click **Save**). Done!

Converting Video into Pictures

Converting video into a series of pictures is even easier. Open a video file and click *File > Save image sequence...*

This window lets you specify the image format produced (**BMP, PNG**, and others) the names of created files, and where the files are placed on the computer. Here's a quick run-through of the essential areas:

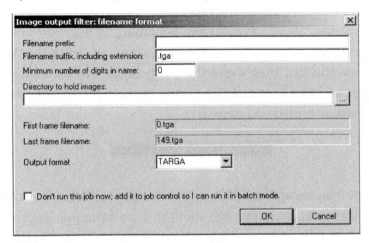

- *Filename prefix* and *Filename suffix:* This lets you specify the first half (prefix) and the last half (suffix) of the image file name. Handy for organizing things.
- *Directory to hold images:* Click the little square with three dots (like this: "...") and find a folder to place the images in.
- *First frame filename* and *Last frame filename:* Shows the names of the first and last images you're about to create.
- *Output format:* Specify what kind of file you want to create. For this example, click and select the "PNG" format.

Click *OK* to exit the window and start the conversion process!

Simple Editing with VirtualDubMod

Some basic editing can be done with VirtualDubMod's simple "timeline" (slider bar). Frames can be deleted (handy if one shows your finger!) and segments of footage can be copied, cut, and pasted.

 The method for selecting several frames is not very obvious. It's done with these two buttons (under the timeline).

To mark the beginning of the selection, move the "playhead" (slider bar) to the first frame, and click the *Mark In* button on the left. Then move the playhead to the last frame in the selection, and click the *Mark Out* button on the right. This selection can be deleted, or copied and pasted.

Many features and capabilities of VirtualDubMod were not explored in this brief tutorial. Learn more about this great program by browsing through the help file, and other resources online. VirtualDubMod will remain a useful tool throughout your moviemaking career!

VirtualDub was written as a way for college student Avery Lee to digitize his anime collection. Several spinoffs of the original project exist, each with their own unique features. Check 'em out!

Links

VirtualDub
    http://www.virtualdub.org/
VirtualDubMod
    http://virtualdubmod.sourceforge.net/

Chapter 15

Sharing Your Animations

Time for the world premiere! Your edit is complete and fans are eager to see your latest film. Successful filmmakers understand it takes hard work and creativity for a film to reach audiences.

Computer Playback

All computers have a media player program that plays audio and video files. Windows programs have Windows Media Player. QuickTime is installed on Macs, (and Windows too, if you've installed iTunes). If you're into free software, check out VLC. These programs are the easiest way to watch animations on the computer they were created on.

Transferring movie files between computers can be complicated. Some files are hundreds of megabytes in size. Many email services reject files this large.

Video compression may solve some of these problems, but the recipient's computer still won't be able to play the video file unless the codec you used to compress the video is installed on their computer. For further information about video codecs, read the **Files and Formats** chapter.

It's best to upload the video file to a video sharing site. This allows others to watch and download the movie in a format that works for them.

Video Sharing Sites

Video sharing websites, like YouTube have become tremendously popular. They are currently the best way to distribute short movies to large audiences, with minimal amount of hassle for the viewer and creator.

Kids, ask your parents for permission before visiting video sharing sites, or creating an account on one.

Video uploaded to a website is converted into a format that can be viewed by anyone with a modern web browser, avoiding the codec hassles, large video files, and all the problems that plagued video sharing in the early days of the Internet.

These sites are simple to use. The video creator creates an account and uploads their video file to the website servers, adding a description of the video and keywords that will enable viewers to find the video with search engines.

The server processes the video, converts it into a new format, typically **Flash video** (**FLV**) and displays the video in the user's profile.

Most video sites have recommended formats and resolutions for uploaded video, and length and filesize restrictions too. The website's upload instructions usually have a recommended procedure to follow.

Short Internet videos are the most successful. Expect your viewers to have short attention spans. You'll grab or lose them in the first two seconds. Opening your movie with titles isn't a good idea, unless they're extremely creative, or contribute to the plot in some way. Save titles for the end of your film.

Releasing films to a public audience entails a knowledge of copyright laws. Most video sharing sites will remove content that is not owned by the uploader, even if they enhanced, or modified the content in some way.

Making DVDs

DVDs are a great way to distribute easy-to-watch copies of your films. If your computer has a DVD burner, it probably came with a software program that creates finished DVDs. The program should have a step-by-step "wizard" or DVD creation process for you to follow. You provide the video file created by your animation software, or exported from your video editing software. The wizard will do the rest.

Computer to TV

You can easily show your animation to a roomful of people by routing your computer display onto a TV screen. A TV can also be used as a second monitor.

Many laptop computers with DVD players have a **VIDEO OUT** port

somewhere. Consult your computer's manual. You may need to visit an electronics retailer or your computer manufacturer to purchase a cable that interfaces with your computer's VIDEO OUT port.

S-Video cables

TVs, DVD players and VCRs have three round connectors. These are called "RCA" or "phono" jacks. The yellow connector is for the video signal, red and white connectors are for audio signals.

"S-Video" connectors are also found in some computers. This is a round connector port with several tiny holes. It may be marked by a picture of a TV screen with a small arrow on it.

If your TV set or DVD player has an S-Video input, you can connect the two with an S-Video cable. If not, you can purchase an "S-Video to Composite" adapter that converts the S-Video plug to an RCA plug.

S-Video to RCA adapter

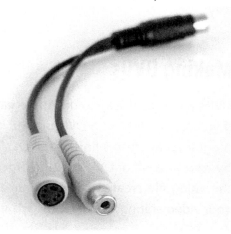

Audio comes out of your computer's headphone jack. You will need a cable to convert this a 1/8 inch "phone plug," into the red and white "RCA" plugs used by TVs. Or, simply play sound through your computer's speakers.

HIGH-DEFINITION MULTIMEDIA INTERFACE

If your computer has an HDMI port, and you have an HD-capable TV that accepts HDMI, the two devices can be connected with an HDMI cable.

An HDMI port. An (unrelated) FireWire port (1394) is pictured immediately to the right.

Copyrights

If you post sound, music, images or video online, or create DVDs and distribute them, ensure you have rights to use the media. This book is not a legal resource, nor is it substitute for advice from a lawyer. However, some great legal resources are available on the web.

- Read books, articles or web sites that explain copyright laws. The Stanford University website has a great introduction to the subject (link at end of chapter)
- Royalty-free music and sound effects can be used in any project after paying a one-time fee.
- If you're a Mac owner, you can compose music with the GarageBand application, bundled with the iLife suite. You own any music created with the software.
- Perform your own compositions, or ask a talented friend to perform for you.
- Ask your favorite artist for permission to use their music in your movie. Sometimes they will say yes, especially if you offer to

credit the performer in your film, or a link to their website. Using properly credited music is publicity for them.

- Use Copyleft and Creative Commons licensed materials. Under these licenses, users may copy and create derivative works, if the results are distributed with the same license.

Links

Stanford University: Copyright and Fair Use Explained
   http://fairuse.stanford.edu/Copyright_and_Fair_Use_Overview/index.html
YouTube
   www.youtube.com
Royalty Free Music
   www.royaltyfreemusic.com
Soundogs (sound effects)
   www.sounddogs.com

Chapter 16

What Next?

Instead of coasting along at a low level of quality or skill, seek to improve your animations by applying new techniques and upgrading your stopmotion studio. Here are some practical suggestions.

Improve Image Quality

A webcam can produce great images, but has its limitations. Higher resolutions, better low-light response, even better focus controls can be found in camcorders, and high-end digital still cameras (DSLRs).

Creating higher-quality animations with a DSLR requires an investment in framegrabbing software that supports a direct link with the camera through USB. This can be done with programs such as **Dragon Stopmotion** for Windows computers, and **iStopmotion** for the Mac. Both programs support a variety of digital still cameras.

Better Lighting

You've been borrowing the lamp off your parent's desk. Drive to an office supply store, visit the lighting aisle, and buy your own desk lamp.

Buy some indoor CFL flood bulbs to use in your lights. Remember to avoid bulbs with a wattage higher than what your lamp accepts.

Get a Table

Find a small table you can use for stopmotion and nothing else. This will allow you to leave your animation setups assembled over a period of days, NOT the time between clearing lunch off the dining room and supper.

Become Literary

Improving the content of your films begins with a deeper knowledge of story structure, story genres, and the subject you are presenting. Start writing your stories down in screenplay format. Read books about screenwriting and story beats. Read screenplays, then watch the film based on the screenplay. How does the director translate the screenplay into visual form?

Act with your Voice

Practice reading stories aloud, giving the characters unique voices. Like a painter uses a brush, the vocal artist creates images with their lungs. Breathing exercises can improve the range and tone of your voice. Here's a simple one.

Breathing Exercise

1. Sit up straight in a chair and look attentive, as if you are gazing at something across the room. Place your hands in your lap, so that your palms rest against your lower abdomen.

2. While sitting like this, breath in slowly and deeply through your nose. Imagine you are filling a balloon, your lungs, to their fullest capacity. Your hands should move out as your lungs fill with air. Keep your chest and shoulders in their normal position as you breath in.

3. After inhaling fully, hold your breath for a moment or two, then exhale slowly through your mouth. Your hands should begin moving in. Concentrate on emptying your lungs from the bottom. Pull your stomach in, tightening your diaphragm muscles. Squeeze every last bit of air from your lungs.

4. All right! You have completed one breathing exercise. Repeat for several minutes. This exercise will strengthen your abdominal muscles and increase your lung capacity. Your voice will strain less as you have more air and breathing control.

Mix your Audio

Stopmotion is audio-intense. As of this writing, the audio capability of most free video editing software is mediocre. To improve the depth and quality of your sound mix, you'll need to invest in pro software, like **Adobe Premiere,** or **Final Cut Express.** Some of the many programs available are listed in the **Editing** chapter.

Buying better audio recording equipment can also improve your production audio. The **Zoom H1,** and **Tascam DR-03,** are great pocket recorders, an inexpensive way to record sound anywhere. Get a mic stand, and use a quality pair of headphones, such as the **Sony MDR-V6** to monitor your audio while recording and editing.

Be a Team Player

While stopmotion can be a solitary basement activity, real filmmaking is never a one-man show. Many people come together to create quality works of art. Taking your productions to the next level means drawing from a wider range of talent. Recruit!

Effects

Spice up your films with post-production effects. Use the techniques we described in the **Flight** and **Fighting** chapters to add greater production values to your projects. While it's possible to create believable effects with free software, acquiring a working knowledge of industry standard software, such as **Adobe After Effects**, is a marketable skill, and might land you a job someday.

Moving On

If you find stopmotion fun, but want to start creating traditional movies in the real world, you can purchase a camera, audio equipment, and basic lighting package. Some investments you've made in software and stopmotion skills will follow you into the new medium, some will not.

Editing

In stopmotion, you stretch the footage you have as far as it will possibly go, recycling and re-arranging frames like a miser. In live-action video, you often have far more footage than is used in the final film. Working with a surplus of footage may be bewildering at first. Much of your time editing will be spent trimming long sections of video into small individual clips.

Sound

In the real world, recording clean audio at the time of filming is essential. Audio recorded outside of a quiet room can be very messy. The best results are achieved with a second microphone, which can be held close to the subject being recorded. Onboard microphones are rarely close enough to the subject to be useful.

Lighting

Three-point lighting techniques are used in stopmotion and real-world applications, but the equipment becomes much larger and heaver. Dealing with the sun and clouds is a constant battle (which animators conveniently avoid in their basement studios).

Cameras

Recording to a MiniDV tape or flash card and downloading the footage to your computer may seem novel after saving your footage to the computer directly. The camera's control menus will share some settings found in your webcam's image controls. Techniques such as **"rack focus"** (when the camera's focus moves between two objects in a shot), **tilts** (tilting the camera up and down) and **pans** (panning the camera left and right) are much easier to apply while the camera is rolling, rather than performing the movement one frame at a time.

Invest in a tripod, but don't be afraid to move the camera off the tripod and around the room between shots, searching for good composition, locking the camera down again when a good frame is found. Unfortunately, many mistake handheld motion for "energy" when it's often an symptom of laziness, an unwillingness to lock the camera down and commit to a shot. Camera movement is good only when it contributes to the story of the film.

An in-depth coverage of video cameras and their features is beyond the scope of this book; however, we encourage you to look for a camera in the "prosumer" range that accepts external audio inputs.

In Conclusion

Films are among the most powerful forms of communication in this age. As a Christian, the author believes that films can be used to communicate the gospel message to audiences.

"And Jesus came and spoke to them, saying, 'All power is given to me in heaven and in earth. Go therefore, and teach all nations, baptizing them in the name of the Father, and of the Son, and of the Holy Ghost: Teaching them to observe all things I have commanded you: and, lo, I am with you always, even to the end of the world'" - **Matthew 28:16-18**

Whatever films you create, think about them not as simple exercises, or random artistic doodles but as expressions of your beliefs.

Become excellent at your craft.

Avoid triviality and mediocrity.

Use your skill for good. And importantly...

Have Fun!

Special Thanks to Amanda, Becky, Emily, Mark, Nathaniel, Rebekah, Rob, Robbie, and Ryan.

Index

A

S

X

CPSIA information can be obtained at www.ICGtesting.com
Printed in the USA
BVOW11s0021081215

429603BV00008B/116/P